Praise for *The Call of Wonder*

"*The Call of Wonder* will rocket you on a mind-bending tour of humanity's consideration of faith, science, and our concepts of God and creation. Brian Cranley helps us consider twin components of human nature: our thirst for the spiritual and our quest to understand the natural universe. Enjoy the ride."

—**TOM JONES**, PhD, veteran NASA astronaut; planetary scientist; author of *Space Shuttle Stories: Firsthand Astronaut Accounts from All 135 Missions*

"What does the starry sky have to do with the human mind? *The Call of Wonder* deftly integrates ancient wisdom with the discoveries of modern science to shed light on how wonder leads us to truth. If you desire to understand reality—and yourself—more fully, pick up this book! It will leave you changed."

—**DR. SOFIA CAROZZA**, postdoctoral research fellow in neuroscience, Harvard Medical School and Brigham & Women's Hospital; published author in *Proceedings of the National Academy of Sciences* and *Psychological Science*

"Brian Cranley invites you to join Sophia, the personification of wisdom, on a beautiful journey from Athens to Jerusalem, from the beginning of the universe to Earth, from the origin of life to the human mind, from Plato to Aquinas, from the shores of the eternal ocean to your own backyard. This is a journey toward truth and wonder, a consilience of science and religion where we find that God is One, that God is Infinite, that God is Eternal, that God is Unknowable."

—**MARTIN NOWAK**, professor of mathematics and biology, Harvard University; author of *Beyond*

THE CALL
of
WONDER

HOW THE
GOD OF REASON
CREATED SCIENCE
IN HIS IMAGE

THE CALL
of
WONDER

BRIAN CRANLEY

GREENLEAF
BOOK GROUP PRESS

Published by Greenleaf Book Group Press
Austin, Texas
www.gbgpress.com

Copyright © 2025 Brian Cranley

All rights reserved.

Thank you for purchasing an authorized edition of this book and for complying with copyright law. No part of this book may be reproduced, stored in a retrieval system, or transmitted by any means, electronic, mechanical, photocopying, recording, or otherwise, without written permission from the copyright holder.

Distributed by Greenleaf Book Group

For ordering information or special discounts for bulk purchases, please contact Greenleaf Book Group at PO Box 91869, Austin, TX 78709, 512.891.6100.

Design and composition by Greenleaf Book Group
Cover design by Greenleaf Book Group
Cover image used under license from ©stock.adobe.com/Mirco Emmy

Publisher's Cataloging-in-Publication data is available.

Print ISBN: 979-8-88645-296-9

eBook ISBN: 979-8-88645-297-6

To offset the number of trees consumed in the printing of our books, Greenleaf donates a portion of the proceeds from each printing to the Arbor Day Foundation. Greenleaf Book Group has replaced over 50,000 trees since 2007.

Printed in the United States of America on acid-free paper

25 26 27 28 29 30 31 32   10 9 8 7 6 5 4 3 2 1

First Edition

*For my girls. The world is a pretty wonderful place.
I love rediscovering it with you.*

CONTENTS

Introduction *1*
Chapter 1: Faith and Science *11*

PART I: The God of Reason

Chapter 2: Plato Begins the Great Conversation *27*
Chapter 3: Aristotle's Everlasting Reply *45*
Chapter 4: The Synthesis of Faith and Reason *63*
Chapter 5: The Image of God *95*

PART II: God's Image in Science

Chapter 6: The Universe *115*
Chapter 7: Life *143*
Chapter 8: The Human Mind *173*

PART III: Further Reflections

Chapter 9: The Scriptures *201*
Chapter 10: The Wonder of It All *229*
Afterword *241*
Two Favors to Ask *245*
Acknowledgments *247*
Notes *249*
About the Author *257*

Introduction

I often go for walks to enjoy the day and clear my head. The neighborhood where I walk is old, but it's undergoing a trendy gentrification due to its proximity to downtown. It has become a great mix of eclectic houses, lush trees, and diverse people.

On one particular day, I noticed new yard signs had popped up in many of the lawns I passed. The signs were all similar, each one worded slightly differently. The gist of the signs went something like this:

In this house, we believe: Love Is Love, All Lives Matter, Women's Rights Are Human Rights, Science Is Real . . .

I stopped halfway through, struck particularly by that one line, *Science Is Real.* I thought to myself, *Who are we talking to here? Are there people out there who think science isn't real?* It quickly dawned on me that the signs were taking a jab at the subset of religious believers who think the findings of modern science contradict their religious beliefs. The people who feel if there is any disagreement between faith and science, then science must be left out altogether as anathema. According to the signs, however, science has the final say. I continued with my walk, but the message continued bothering me. So much for clearing my head.

My Journey

The realization that faith and science may have a real chance to coexist happened slowly for me, over the span of twenty-five years and well after studying for degrees on both sides. During my undergraduate at Texas A&M University, I majored in the hard sciences, pursuing a bachelor's in biomedical engineering. There I learned the basics of biology, as well as more physics and math than I could ever want to know. It was during this time a love for the discoveries of space and the origins of the universe also began to bloom. I was continually fascinated by the images of deep space produced by the Hubble telescope, as well as the findings from high-speed particle collisions coming out of the Large Hadron Collider in Switzerland. Nerdy stuff.

After I graduated college, my life took a very different course. Struck by what I felt was a higher calling, I left my job as an engineer to study philosophy and theology for future ministry at the University of Dallas and the University of St. Thomas in Houston. It was during this period that I fell in love with the ideas put forth from the Greek masters, Plato and Aristotle. It amazed me how these ancients distilled so much truth about the universe from simple observation and communal discourse.

I also found myself drawn to the ideas of divinity introduced during the medieval scholastic period. Thinkers like Thomas Aquinas fascinated me with their precise and logical approach to the study of God and faith, a field not often associated with scrupulous thinking. It was as if they were using the scientific method on the higher things of God, a perspective I could relate with from my undergrad days.

Looking back now, I can see *wonder* was calling to me through both disciplines. I felt it when looking at the images of deep space, and I encountered a similar experience when reading Plato's description of the Form of the Good. Looking up into a star-filled night sky began to feel oddly similar to looking up into a fresco-filled cathedral dome. It wouldn't be until ten years or so after my studies, however, that wonder would bring these two fields together in an extraordinary way.

I distinctly remember the day faith and science came together in a way that changed me forever. I was hoping to relax with something interesting after a normal day at work. I settled on a YouTube video titled "What Happened before the Big Bang?" put out by Fermilab, the particle physics laboratory in Chicago. It focused on what happened at the origin of the universe, a topic that always strikes me as fascinating. I listened casually as the video explained how in the very first moment of time all things were just *one* thing.

We are familiar today with mass, energy, and the forces that govern physics, but in the very beginning, the video said, this familiarity was likely not so. My curiosity was piqued. The video went on to emphasize that, in the universe's very first moment, the unity of things was so great even the four forces of physics may have all been one and the same thing.

No differentiations. A perfect unity.

Wonder hit me like a brick in the face. My philosophy and theology studies came flooding back, forming a thought clearly in my mind.

God has written His image into the very science of the universe.

Every author has their biases and in that regard I am not exempt. At the outset, I feel it's important to let you know where I stand in terms of my own beliefs. I believe in Christianity and I prefer the more ancient expressions of the faith. But as C. S. Lewis says in the preface of *Mere Christianity*, "In this book, I'm not trying to convert anyone to my own position."[1] Rather, in this book I hope to join the centuries-old discussion of how a rational belief in God can coexist with a love for scientific discovery. In that way, the book is more a defense of monotheism than of Christianity alone.

I am keenly aware that my personal beliefs have colored everything I've written here, but I don't think there is any way around that. I was trained in the Western, Catholic tradition where I learned to love the gift of rational faith and the preservation of ancient heritage. Many of the ideas in this book come directly from that education. I've studied a bit of Eastern Orthodox Christianity, where I learned to love God as mystery and gained a deep appreciation of that mystery in the art form of iconography. In my studies and experiences of Protestant Christianity, I have come to revere their emphasis on Scripture study and cultivating a personal relationship with Jesus.

To Judaism, I owe a debt of gratitude for their original faithfulness to the call of God and for the preservation of the Hebrew Scriptures, which served as the foundation for most of monotheism. As for my studies and friendships in Islam, I am grateful for their emphasis on living a life of submission to the will of Allah and for their public commitment to prayer five times daily. Finally, I have learned a lot from my atheist and agnostic friends who authentically seek the truth of things. Through them, I have come to a greater appreciation of the sciences and the wonder of the world right before our eyes. I recognize that my life and beliefs have been colored by a variety of sources and I am thankful for having experienced all of it. That being said, let's now return to the topic at hand.

Climbing the Mountain

I have a friend, Tim, who is something of an adventure junkie. Every six months or so he'll say something to the effect of, "Man, it's been too long, I gotta get back out there." By now I know what he means. He absolutely loves being outdoors and traveling to new, exotic locations. Mix in some adventure and an adrenaline rush and it's a perfect trip. Tim has camped out in the Utah mountains in sub-zero conditions. He's backpacked across Kauai, the wildest of the Hawaiian Islands, and he's currently planning trips to the mountain ruins of Machu Picchu in Peru, as well as the remote wilderness of Patagonia in Chile. Tim tells me whenever he's out in the raw beauty of nature is when he feels most alive. It's his place to find wonder, and I get it. In fact, if I'm being honest, I'm a little jealous of him.

A few years ago, I finally decided to join Tim on one of these adventures. He had lived in Colorado for some time and had always wanted to climb Longs Peak along the famous Keyhole Route, as it's the only fourteener (a mountain peak with an elevation of at least 14,000 feet) you can see from Denver. Tim spent so many years staring at this mountain he said it "called to him" to come and attempt a climb.

The thing about Longs Peak is that it's not a beginner fourteener. If you don't regularly climb mountains, it can be a serious challenge—dangerous even. To put things in perspective, I live in sea-level Texas and do not regularly climb anything. The National Park Service's brochure describes Longs Keyhole Route this way:

> **The Keyhole Route is NOT a hike!** It is a climb that crosses enormous sheer vertical rock faces, often with falling rocks, requiring scrambling, where an unroped fall would likely be fatal. The route has narrow ledges, loose rock, and steep cliffs. The terrain requires good route-finding and scrambling skills. Use caution, as injuries requiring rescue are very dangerous and take many hours, if not days, to execute.[2]

Needless to say, it was a perfect trip for Tim and a daunting challenge for me. I was both excited and anxious as we prepared for months before embarking on the hike.

Finally, the day came. We set out from Denver joined by Tim's friend, Jason, who was also experienced in the mountains. The initial hike up Longs Peak lived up to its name. It was very, very *long*. It was also filled with fantastic views of the Rocky Mountains. The higher we climbed, the more incredible the sights became. Tim had the foresight to reserve us a campsite near the Keyhole rock formation, where we stayed the night in tents, utterly exhausted. Very early the next morning, the three of us started off through the Keyhole rested and ready to go for the summit.

The Keyhole rock itself is a huge hole in a section of granite that sits high upon the ridgeline. It marks the divide between one side of the mountain from the other and identifies a change in the trail from a slow and steady hike to more serious scrambling. When your body passes through the Keyhole, the wind comes rushing up the far side of the mountain and blasts you in the face. The gale is so strong it feels like you might be blown off the mountain altogether. You can see for miles, but you also see that this new side of the mountain is much steeper than the side you just came up on.

We were lucky to have beautiful weather on the day of our summit attempt, but the going was difficult. At one time or another, each of us considered turning back, but after pausing for a breath and summoning some courage, we pushed on. We went over the narrows with sheer, thousand-foot drops, climbed up the seemingly endless boulder wall with loose rocks ready to fall. Finally, using our hands and feet, we scrambled up the home stretch until we reached the top. Once there, the 360-degree view was even more breathtaking than expected. Even better than the view was the sense of accomplishment, camaraderie, and wonder that accompanied it.

Reflecting back on the experience now, I am still struck by the overwhelming sense of awe that the rugged beauty of a 14,000-foot mountain can bring. Just standing in the strength of its presence made me feel small and humbled. The mountain commanded our respect without having to do anything at all, simply by being immovably present. The experience of the climb was one of real wonder, something I continue to seek more of to this day.

Wonder

Our world is full of various types of wonder, some more satiating than others. There seems to be a barrage of cheap wonder these days with the onset of modern media. I'm thinking here of the quick highs that come from scrolling social media clips with titles like "The Craziest Thing You've Ever Seen!!!" or over-the-top CGI action movies that bombard the senses for three hours straight. It's all very exciting, it's entertaining, but the thrill is soon over and often leaves us with the regret of time wasted. This is not the type of wonder I'm after any longer.

A second form of wonder comes from using the imagination. Our imagination is a powerful instrument capable of conjuring up all kinds of excitement. With it we can envision a magnificent future for ourselves, one that's overflowing with success, love, and happiness. Children use it to dream up a myriad of games and spend countless hours playing under its spell.

While the imagination is a helpful tool for growth and creativity when used wisely, it can also become a shackle if allowed to go unchecked. Some people are unable to leave the world of their imagination and so end up missing out on the life right in front of them. I'm thinking here of those we know stuck in the glory days of their past or the dreamers who want a better life for themselves but never take the first action step to get there. Imagination can bring wonder, but, again, it's not the type of wonder I want anymore.

What I'm looking for is something I call *authentic* wonder. It is the experience that comes when we make ourselves present to bigger realities. Big things—like the vastness of space, the beauty of nature, or the existence of God. It occurs when we ponder things that are outside of ourselves.

Authentic wonder is a transformative force. When encountered, it provides immediate perspective of our place in the larger picture and it quiets the soul with stillness. It is the type of wonder I see on my daughters' faces when they watch the otters playing at the zoo or marvel at a lunar eclipse as it dims out the sun. It's the experience my classmate had when hearing Aristotle's argument that a divine being must necessarily be unchanging and therefore exist outside of time. And it is the wonder I found at the top of a long hike up a fourteener in the rugged nature of the Rockies. Astonishingly, this type of wonder is readily accessible; sometimes, we just need to be reminded of where to find it.

The Invitation

As we begin this journey through philosophy, theology, cosmology, and biology, I would like to offer an invitation. If you find yourself on the side of science and have difficulty with the idea of an old man with a white beard floating around up in the sky, let your mind take in the more rational ideas of divinity from philosophers like Plato, Aristotle, and Aquinas. Allow yourself to absorb an ancient perspective on God you may not have heard before. The description of God arrived at via logic and natural reasoning.

On the other hand, if you find yourself on the side of faith, and science seems like a scary proposition, I invite you to take the time to savor the wonders of modern scientific discovery. Let yourself bask in the beauty and awe of the physical world, as discovered in recent centuries by men and women who've devoted their lives to the task. These mysteries of science may open your mind to new perspectives on how the universe can be a source of revelation all its own.

In Part I, we will explore the lines of ancient thought, from philosophy and theology, that used natural reason to arrive at a rational description of God. We'll consider ideas from the ancient Greeks through Plato and his pupil Aristotle, and then we'll discuss how subsequent philosophers synthesized the work of the Greeks into the faiths of Judaism, Islam, and Christianity through several prominent figures.

In Part II, we will delve deeper into the three miracles of modern science to see how science is discovering the very same

God in its own way. We will look at how the Big Bang, the evolution of life, and the mystery of the human mind each reveal the image of God from Part I of the book. We will journey through the beauty of the universe and the diversity of biological life, ending with a look inside the human rational mind that sets us apart from everything else in the world.

Lastly, in Part III, we will discover how the rational image of God revealed in philosophy and science can also be found in the sacred Scriptures.

One final note: At the beginning of each chapter, I have written a short fable meant to serve three purposes. First, to provide a mental break as we cover some fairly in-depth content in the chapters. Second, to set the stage historically for the content that will follow. Third, and most importantly, to communicate the *experience* of what it feels like to discover timeless truths from a variety of sources. At least, what it felt like for me when I learned them.

My hope is that this journey will provide you with new ideas to savor as well as some real experiences of authentic wonder along the way. Most of all, I hope to share how, for me, faith and science have become two sides of the same reality.

Welcome to the journey.

CHAPTER 1

Faith and Science

"Wisdom begins in wonder."

—Socrates

Fable

You are walking on a city sidewalk late in the afternoon as the sun sits low in the sky, casting an orange glow on the surrounding structures. There's no one else around, just you and your thoughts. As you pass by an office building with its brown brick and bland windows, the front door bursts open and a woman wearing a long pale dress walks out. Her appearance is striking with silver hair, penetrating eyes, and skin that looks almost golden. You have a hard time discerning her age or her descent.

She looks directly at you and says, "We are in need of assistance; will you come with me?"

Taken aback by the abrupt appearance of this mysterious woman and even more so by her bold request, you consider the situation. On one hand, there isn't anywhere you need to be this evening. On the other, who knows what awaits inside that building? Something intrigues you about this woman, however, so you decide to offer your assistance.

"Sure. I'm not sure how I can help, but I'll try."

Inside, the woman seems to glide down the hall, leading you through a dimly lit corridor to a set of double doors. You can hear the murmur of voices and the shuffling of chairs coming from inside. Your host opens the doors into a large conference room filled with a dozen people seated around a large oval-shaped, mahogany table. A row of windows along the wall on one side lets in the light from a fading sunset. At first glance, some of the faces in the room strike you as familiar but difficult to place in your memory. Strangely, most of the people are dressed in clothing from a long-gone antiquity. You think to yourself, *What have I gotten myself into?*

Side conversations die down as your host moves to the head of the table, directing you to sit beside her in an empty chair. Once the room is silent, she begins to address the group. "Welcome, everyone. I have called this meeting to discuss some of the foundational realities of our world. A big task to be sure. My new friend here"—she gestures toward you with her hand and nods—"has graciously agreed to aid us in recording the meeting minutes and finer points of our discussion." The person next to you slides over a large, worn leather notebook, cracking with age, and a box of pens.

The realization of what you've just agreed to starts to set in. With growing disdain, you think, *I've given up my night to be a meeting scribe.*

The host resumes, "As all of you know, but our guest does not, I am Sophia. I have called each of you here tonight and am eager to begin this long-awaited discussion." She looks to her left and continues the introductions, moving clockwise around the table.

"Plato and Aristotle are here representing their field of ancient Greek philosophy. Next to them we have Philo of Alexandria and Moses Maimonides joining on behalf of Judaism and Jewish theology. Ibn Sina and Ibn Rush'd are here representing the Golden Age of Islam. Next to them are Augustine of Hippo and Thomas Aquinas with Christian Scholasticism."

Your mind is racing. *Did she just say Plato and Aristotle? As in the guys from centuries ago?*

Sophia pauses for a moment to let the group settle. "Albert Einstein and Edwin Hubble are here on behalf of our knowledge of space, time, and the universe. And last but certainly not least, we have Charles Darwin and Mary Anning as representatives of the wonders of biologic life and the natural world."

You can't believe what you're hearing; these men and women are dead and gone, some for a very long time. You attempt to calm your mind, then decide to stop trying to figure it out. If this meeting and these people are real, perhaps taking notes from their discussion may not be so bad after all.

Sophia offers guidance for the structure of the conversation. "Each person will be given a chance to speak on their life's work, focusing on a few specific areas of expertise. Next, each pair of representatives will present the major findings from their respective fields, including contributions their field has made to the overall body of human thought." Sophia sits, points to Plato, and nods.

It begins.

As Plato speaks, you are drawn in by the wisdom of his words. Aristotle and the others provide equally fascinating material. The meeting stretches on and the light outside fades into a deep black. You can't write fast enough as the pages of the notebook fill up. All your previous thoughts of a wasted evening are gone. Whatever this is, it's real.

Your mind tries to comprehend the ideas shared. It feels like your brain could explode at any moment, crammed with challenging concepts. At the same time, there is a sense of fulfillment welling up within you. You don't really want this to end, so you listen and write as best you can.

The light from overhead catches on your watch face and you see it's now two in the morning—the night has flown by. You're tired and your hand is cramping badly, and still the people speak. Finally, as Charles Darwin and Mary Anning conclude explanations on the beauty of nature, Sophia calls for a brief break.

The attendees mull about, carrying on side discussions. Plato and Aquinas debate by the watercooler, playing with its knobs and filling cups in amazement. Ibn Rush'd and Moses Maimonides corner Aristotle and press him with questions. Einstein and Augustine sit in a corner talking animatedly with their hands.

Sophia takes a moment to check in, turning to you.

"How are things going?"

"Very well. I've never heard these topics discussed like this before."

"Good to hear. I'm so glad you could join us," she says.

Sophia calls the meeting back together and announces a final portion of the discussion as everyone returns to their seats. "For this last part, each pair of representatives will share their observations on the other groups' fields of study."

You think to yourself, *What on earth does Greek philosophy have in common with Einstein's theory of relativity and outer space? And how will Charles Darwin comment on the nature of divinity that the three groups of theologians presented so passionately?*

Right when you thought the discussion was winding down, you realize the best part has only just begun. The conversation flows on. Your mind is overloaded with new insights, with connections you've never considered before. As the rays of the early morning sun creep over the edge of the windowsills, Sophia finally calls the meeting to an end. While your hand cannot write a single word more, you're struck by the solemnity of this gathering.

For the first time since entering the room, you speak up. "Do we have to stop? What if we take another short break and continue a bit longer?"

"Unfortunately," Sophia replies, "we cannot. The sun has risen and now we must go."

You say your goodbyes to the group, trying to smile amid the disappointment. Each person thanks you for your efforts and your host escorts you back to the front door.

"Thank you, really. You've been a great help." Sophia smiles. "Goodbye for now."

She turns and you watch as the door closes behind her. The brightness of the morning sun blinds your eyes as you wander aimlessly down the sidewalk. *What the heck just happened?* Though it was hard work and you're physically exhausted, you feel a sense of inner peace and mental satisfaction.

As you make your way home, you begin to relax and something falls from your grip, hitting the concrete. *The notebook! All those notes for Sophia.*

You run back to the office building, hoping to catch her before she's gone. Panting heavily, a stitch in your side and sweat under your arms, you open the front door and race down the hall to the meeting room. When you swing open the inner doors, the room is empty. Dust lies on the table and you find no trace of any meeting. You call down the hall, but your echo is the only reply. You feel terrible about forgetting to leave the notes.

Setting the notebook down on the table, you flip through its pages, pondering what to do next. The notes are captivating. The whole thing reminds you of a treasure map leading to a secret of inestimable value. As you stand there reading, one word comes to mind as a perfect summary of what you are experiencing.

Wonder.

The Great Divide

Too many people today view belief in God and belief in science as contradictory. Modern thinking claims they are oil and water, incompatible forever and always. In a 2010 interview with ABC's Diane Sawyer, the famous astrophysicist Stephen Hawking put it this way: "There is a fundamental difference between religion, which is based on authority, and science, which is based on observation and reason."[1] For clarification, a fundamental difference is one that can never be reconciled.

Many of us are taught from a young age that if we are religious, we must reject the discoveries of science. On the other hand, if we believe in science, we must push away our faith in a higher power as the naïve myths of childhood. This rather serious problem divides us both from within ourselves and within our human community in a real way. The division can turn attempts at rational discourse into angry battles of faith versus science—as both communities are equally passionate about their beliefs.

I have watched the divide between faith and science grow larger over the years. My good friends who love science no longer attend church, and I don't necessarily blame them. After speaking with them at great length, I've realized that the description of

God they were given as children simply contradicts their rational, adult mind. A rational mind that science now seems to satiate with greater fulfillment.

On the other hand, I have other friends who hold their faith so dear they feel the need to reject modern science altogether. Because it can be difficult to reconcile the discoveries of science with the stories of our sacred texts, some believers have decided to let science go completely and cling to God in a purity of faith. I will admit I admire their commitment and adherence to what they believe to be true.

Perhaps more importantly, I've experienced this divide within myself. I was raised in a devout Christian home where I was taught to accept God as the ultimate reality. It wasn't until my natural interests in science and physics began to bloom that I started questioning what I had previously believed to be true. I remember going through long periods of believing strongly in faith and mentally "pushing out" ideas like the Big Bang and biologic evolution. Then, after meandering back into the world of science out of genuine curiosity, I would mentally force myself to accept the scientific description of things and "push out" the stories of faith as the vestiges of a lost, ancient world.

The process went on like this for many years until it became something of an internal obsession for me. I remember thinking to myself, *If faith and science are both true, then logically speaking, they must be reconcilable.*

In his wisdom, my dad taught us something that has helped more than anything in my attempt to reconcile the two sides. He told us that every great mystery holds two seemingly opposed sides in tension. To find the truth, you cannot let go of either side. You must "hang there on the cross," in long suffering, between the two, until the truth in the middle is revealed.

He promised us that the truth we found would be something new, something we hadn't considered before. He also said that the newly discovered truth would be greater than either of the two sides alone. In other words, a "synergistic truth" in the spirit of Stephen Covey's 7 *Habits of Highly Effective People*.[2] Wise words indeed. And so, I spent most of my young adult life shifting back and forth between faith on the one hand and science on the other, trying my best to remember the words of my father whenever I grew tired of the tension and pushed one side away.

The Cognitive Dissonance Is Real

From the time we enter public school, we learn that science is rooted in reason and we should only believe in what we can see. On the other hand, we learn from our religious journeys that faith is about believing what we cannot see. It's difficult because faith and science both claim to reveal the truth. However, at face value, they seem to reveal two very different truths. For most of us, it remains a struggle to merge the peace-inducing thoughts of a loving God with the cold, hard facts of science.

The issue gets much more serious when the disconnect between these two sides leads individuals to feel they must choose one or the other. We end up buying into the either/or dichotomy about faith and science because the human mind has trouble maintaining two beliefs we feel to be contradictory. This is a phenomenon known as cognitive dissonance.

Cognitive dissonance describes the feeling that arises when we try to entertain two conflicting notions. To alleviate this unsettling experience, we often suppress one thought in favor of the other. This allows us to maintain a consistent internal narrative. If you firmly believe yourself to be a great golfer, but you consistently kick your golf ball out of a difficult lie, you will experience a sense of inner conflict. Are you really as good as you think you are? To resolve this, your mind may excuse your poor performance as an unlucky streak or just a bad day. It is not possible for you to believe that you are both a great golfer and a terrible one at the same time.

In his seminal 1956 book, *When Prophecy Fails*, psychologist Leon Festinger illustrates the lengths to which people will go to continue believing what they've already decided is true.[3] Festinger observes how members of doomsday cults deal with the fact that the world didn't end when they thought it would. He notes many fervent believers continue to convince themselves that the next time will be for real, even in the wake of failed prophecies. To maintain this strong sense of belief, it's necessary for these true believers to embrace their faith even if it means ignoring scientific evidence that suggests what they're predicting can't possibly happen.

The groups Festinger observed showed an intense dedication to their faith, despite all scientific evidence that what they believed didn't make sense. He found that the true believers didn't adjust to the new reality by accepting they were wrong. Instead, they rationalized the continuation of life on Earth as a mere miscalculation. The more invested a member of the group was, the less willing they were to admit their faith misled them. While doomsday cults are the extreme example, most of us would agree that we tend to hold our religious beliefs dear.

To add to the confusion, events sometimes occur on the global stage that fuels the perception that religion and science are irreconcilable. In 1633, for example, Galileo was declared "vehemently suspect of heresy" and sentenced to house arrest by the Catholic Church for proclaiming the Copernican belief that the earth revolved around the sun. After much discernment, the Church has since come to adopt a modern view of our place in the cosmos, one that correlates with the observations of science, but that event helped create the public perception that faith and science are naturally opposed.

Take as another example, the 1987 Supreme Court case of Edwards vs. Aguillard where the court ruled 7–2 against a Louisiana law requiring creation science to be taught in public schools whenever evolutionary science was taught. This case set a national precedent that belief in creationism belongs in the church while belief in evolution belongs in the classroom. These events, along with others, have led people to believe the more you favor one side, the less you can hold on to the other.

The pressure to buy into the either/or dichotomy affected many of history's greatest thinkers. One of these was the man whose theory of evolution rocked the world: Charles Darwin. Darwin (1809–1882) began his life as a Christian, and even briefly studied to become a clergyman in the Anglican Church. Over the course of his research, however, Darwin had trouble with the dissonance he felt between his old faith and his new scientific theory. Questions directed to him about his personal beliefs exerted a steady pressure over the years, and the cognitive dissonance he felt led Darwin toward agnosticism—the belief that we can never know whether or not God exists. He likely struggled with the tension all his life and, while leaning toward full-on atheism, he never completely let go of a belief in God.

We can see the tension clearly in his personal writings. In some cases, he writes of a need for a Creator, and in others, he writes of the lack of proof he finds in supporting religious claims. Nick Spencer, author of *Darwin and God*, describes this conflict in an article he wrote for The Faraday Institute:

Although fluctuating throughout the period, [Darwin] was, ultimately, happiest with the label agnostic, a word newly minted by his friend, Thomas Henry Huxley. "The mind refuses to look at this universe, being what it is, without having been designed," he wrote to Frances Wedgewood in 1861. "Yet, where one would most expect design, viz. in the structure of a sentient being, the more I think on the subject, the less I can see proof of design." "I am driven to two opposite conclusions," he admitted to Henry Acland. "My theology is a simple muddle," he told Joseph Hooker.[4]

On the other side, there is the hero of the Reformation, Martin Luther, who struggled to accept the legitimacy of science and human reason. As the father of Protestant Christianity, Luther is one of the most consequential religious figures in Western history. In 1546, he gave his last sermon as the dean of theology of the University of Wittenberg just three days before his death. In a final act of admonition, Luther preached the following:

> Usury, gluttony, adultery, manslaughter, murder, etc., these can be seen and the world understands that these are sins. But since the devil's bride, reason, the lovely whore, comes in and wants to be wise, and what she says, she thinks, is the Holy Spirit. Who can be of any help then? Neither jurist, physician, nor king, nor emperor; for she [reason] is the foremost whore the devil has. The other gross sins can be seen, but nobody can control reason.[5]

Martin Luther also spoke out against Copernicus's theory of heliocentrism, the idea that the earth revolves around the sun.

He favored the traditional belief of geocentrism, that the earth is the center of the universe, because it supported the ideas found in Genesis that God made the earth as the center of His creative work. Statements like these have given Luther a reputation for being anti-science, though, as we all know, it is never that black and white. In other places, Luther spoke highly of astronomers as being masters of their field and praised the scientific study of nature because its beauty gives greater glory to God.

Both Darwin and Luther illustrate the either/or dichotomy people feel when considering how to best live a faith-filled life, or a rational, scientific one. The good news is this separation might not be necessary at all. We are often taught to believe faith and science are dissonant, but perhaps they don't have to be.

History shows that the hard sciences were often fostered and preserved within religious institutions. For this reason, there were many historical figures who believed in both God and science. Sir Isaac Newton (1643–1727), for instance, believed strongly in God. He saw his work as an uncovering of the laws of nature that God put into place. Newton is famous for his work in physics, but he also spent a considerable amount of personal time writing on matters of theology. A quote often attributed to him is, "Gravity explains the motions of the planets, but it cannot explain who set the planets in motion. God governs all things and knows all that is or can be done." As if to double down on his beliefs in both science and God, in the "General Scholium" he added to his second edition of the *Principia*, he writes, "This most beautiful system of the sun, planets and comets, could only proceed from the counsel and dominion of an intelligent and powerful Being."[6] The struggle to reconcile faith and science as Isaac Newton seems to have done is not an easy one. It remains one of the biggest challenges each of us must face.

A quick search on the internet reveals the status of the faith versus science divide today. Millions of results appear for videos of believers debating atheists on the existence of God. Unfortunately, the discourse reflected in these debates isn't always open-minded and civil. There's a successful Christian movie franchise, *God's Not Dead*, based on the premise that atheist college professors are forcing believing students to abandon their religion altogether or risk failing their class. The divide between faith and science is alive and well, both inside our individual minds and within our greater human community. I'd like to believe, however, that there's still a good majority of people out there who are honestly just seeking the truth of the matter.

Two things have helped me tremendously in finding a reconciliation between the worlds of faith and science. The first is the experience of wonder, and the second is the common language of logic and reason. I felt wonder for a long time while learning about natural biology and deep space. It wasn't until I heard God described by the ancients in logical terms that I also began to experience wonder in the world of faith. That rational description of God, formed over thousands of years by many of history's greatest minds, is where we turn to now in the next chapters.

PART I

The God of Reason

CHAPTER 2

Plato Begins the Great Conversation

"We can easily forgive a child who is afraid of the dark; the real tragedy of life is when men are afraid of the light."

—Plato

Fable

Athens, Greece. You've wanted to make this trip for a long time, and now, here you are. The Greek isles are well known for their beautiful blue waters, pristine beaches, delicious foods, and unique culture. You are in the capital city of Athens—particularly famous for its strong influence on the history of Western thought. It is often referred to as an incubator for some of the greatest philosophical minds the world has ever known.

You are standing atop the Acropolis, or "high city," that offers a 360-degree view of modern Athens below. The ancient Greek structures surrounding you are mesmerizing, their walls packed with centuries of history. You overhear from a nearby tour guide that the Acropolis dates back to the Neolithic period, around 5000 BC. It is set upon a giant limestone plateau, which, itself, dates back even further, to the Cretaceous period, when dinosaurs still roamed the earth.

The most iconic of the Acropolis buildings is the famed Parthenon—a huge, Doric-style structure made entirely of columns supporting an ornate roof. It was originally created as a temple for the Greek goddess Athena, after whom the city of Athens is named. Since its construction, the Parthenon has served as a temple, a castle, a political theater, a church, a mosque, and an army barracks. Though ancient enemies and the ravages of time have left it in ruins, even now it remains the most recognizable sight in all of Greece.

As you finish taking in the scenic beauty and rich history, you decide to head back into the bustling metropolis of modern-day Athens. You walk down the steep hill of the Acropolis and then through winding streets and open-air markets, enjoying the local life with all its sights and smells.

Crossing through a crowded plaza, you feel someone take your hand. Surprised, you look up to find Sophia smiling back at you. It's been over a year since your encounter at the office building, but the wonder of that evening has stayed with you ever since. In fact, it's one of the reasons you chose to vacation in Athens.

"Hello again," Sophia says warmly. "If you'd like, you can come with me; there are some friends I'd love for you to see."

"Well, hello again! Of course, I would love to." Your steps grow faster with anticipation as she leads you off in a new direction.

You begin eagerly telling her all the things you've been thinking about since the meeting. She listens while guiding you through a dark alleyway between two buildings. You emerge out of the other side and back into the bright sunlight.

As your eyes readjust to the light, you look around and realize things are very different now. "Wait, are we still in Athens?"

Sophia laughs. "Yes, this is still Athens. But this is the Athens of 350 BC."

Your eyes widen and your jaw drops. *Impossible.*

You follow Sophia through the ancient city, admiring the original stone pathways and old Greek architecture. For the most part, the people look the same, dark hair and prominent features, though many are dressed in the stereotypical Greek tunic and cloak.

Walking along, you notice a group engaged in the construction of a small building. The two of you stop briefly to observe. Two men are working to create a mixture of clay, water, and straw. After the mixing is complete, they transfer the sticky substance to others waiting near an empty rectangle constructed of wood. They pack the clay mixture tightly into the wooden form until it assumes the shape of a block. Then they leave it to dry in the sun, moving on to start the next one.

Interesting, you think to yourself.

Sophia leads you on from the workers and you walk for a while past the bulk of the buildings until you reach a clearing on the edge of the city. This area is filled with trees and pathways much like a city park. As you come through a patch of dense shrubs, you see another group sitting on stone benches. The group is focused intently on two individuals standing up front about to address the gathering.

Getting closer, you realize you know the two men up front. You recognize them from the meeting last year with Sophia. The older man with broad shoulders and full gray beard is Plato. The younger one next to him is Aristotle, whose beard still retains its youthful color. The group seated around them waits with anticipation for them to speak.

Sophia takes a seat on one of the benches near the back. She leans over and whispers, "Welcome to the Academy of Athens. Sit here and listen; I will translate for you."

"I recognize those two," you whisper back excitedly.

"Pay close attention; you are witnessing the beginning of one of the greatest discussions ever conducted. This conversation will continue from here, through the centuries, for a very long time to come."

You remain standing for a moment, still stunned by the realization of where you are, then take your seat next to Sophia and prepare to soak it all in . . . again.

Plato and the Theory of Forms

Our journey into the image of God by way of human reason begins back in ancient Athens with Plato, one of the most iconic of the philosophers. Technically speaking, the great conversation began long before Plato as Plato himself was taught by Socrates and Socrates by Anaxagoras and so on. It is Plato's dialogues that have come down to us, however, and within those writings we find Socrates, his teacher, always portrayed as the main character. In

Plato's writings, then, we also receive the thought of those great minds who came before him. So, for the sake of simplicity, we will attribute the beginning of the great conversation concerning the God of reason to Plato.

In his own right, Plato is widely considered one of the most influential thinkers in Western thought, so powerfully did his ideas transform the subjects they touched. The philosopher and mathematician Alfred North Whitehead went so far as to say that Plato set the agenda for the rest of Western philosophy that was to follow. Plato was born in Athens around the years 429–423 BC, the exact date being unknown. He belonged to an aristocratic, well-to-do family, with a pedigree spanning back to the early kings of Athens. As a young man, he excelled in all aspects of school, as well as athletics, particularly enjoying the sport of wrestling. The name Plato was likely a nickname from the word *platon*, meaning "broad," referring to his large, broad-shouldered stature.

As a youth, Plato traveled extensively. While visiting places like Italy, Sicily, and Egypt, he often sought out the most learned teachers to absorb local thoughts on politics, life, and wisdom in general. Many believe it was these travels—and the corresponding diversity of knowledge acquired—that gave Plato such a profound insight into universal principles applicable to all times and cultures.

One such universal principle for which Plato is known is the theory of forms. The theory claims there exists an unseen, immaterial world of ideal things (forms). Plato argues that the forms are the most real things of all; however, these forms are nonphysical and therefore inaccessible to our senses. It is through our reason alone that we gain access to this higher world of forms.

In the perfect world of forms, there exists the ideal template of everything here in the normal, physical world. Think of an ideal cookie cutter from which many individual things are shaped. For Plato, reality has a hierarchy of being and the forms occupy the highest place. They are perfect in themselves, ideal archetypes and uncorrupted in any way. The things we encounter through our senses derive their being from the forms. As the "most real things of all," the forms are actually the things themselves and not just a mold for the copies in the physical world.

Below the forms in Plato's hierarchy comes the physical world. Everyday things like people, plants, and animals are imperfect in some way compared to the perfection of the form from which they come. For Plato, there is always a blemish or deformity found in physical things, making them less than perfect.

Let's look at the example of common horses. We know that an Arabian and a Clydesdale are both horses. But how is it we know this specific animal is a horse, and that other animal is a horse, but the mountain over there is not a horse? The theory of the forms says it's because there is an ideal form of *horse-ness* that informs our minds with the template to recognize a horse when we see one. From this template, we can correctly apply the concept of horse to each different horse we encounter in the world.

Another way to look at the example is to say that every physical horse "participates" in the ideal form of horse-ness. The universal forms have a real impact on the physical world for Plato. They underlie every physical thing and they help our minds to know what different things are. Plato's philosophy defines the form of horse-ness as "what it means to be a horse." He taught that it is the form that gives existence and meaning to every physical horse participating in it. Plants participate in the form of plant-ness, houses participate in the form of house-ness, and humans participate in the ideal form of what it means to be a human. There is an ideal version of every different thing we know here in the physical world existing in the unseen world of the forms.

The universal forms are not limited to physical objects alone. Values and virtues, likewise, have their ideal representations in the world of the forms. Invisible notions such as truth, beauty, and justice each have their own ideal template. Take, for instance, the virtue of courage. Courage is nonphysical and can only be "seen" occurring within human actions. It is observed in the way humans react to given situations. To stand against all odds for something one believes in deeply is considered an act of courage. The courage itself may be invisible, but that does not make it any less real for Plato. So it is with other virtues like justice, temperance, and so on. To be an ideal human is to act in accordance with these ideal forms of the human virtues.

Below physical things on Plato's hierarchy of being, we reach the bottom. Here we find the images and representations of physical objects. Think here of photographs, paintings, and shadows. These are not actual things but merely their representations. Plato puts them in the lowest place because they are the furthest removed from the most real things of all—the forms.

Plato's hierarchy is a pyramid of sorts. At the base, we have the representations of physical things. On the second tier, we find the physical things themselves, and at the top come the perfect ideal forms. As we ascend the hierarchy of being, we also move from the many to the few. There are an infinite number of representations of physical things, there are fewer actual physical things, and there are even fewer ideal forms.

Interestingly, the top level of forms contains a second hierarchy within it as well. The forms are divided into three layers: the lower forms, the higher forms, and on top is the one form to rule them all. The lower forms comprise the ideal versions of physical objects like mountains and horses. The higher forms are those of values and virtues, such as truth, beauty, and so on. At the very top of the pyramid, we find the one most important form of all, something Plato calls the Form of the Good.

THE FORM OF THE GOOD

At the very top of Plato's pyramid of forms, there sits the Form of the Good. It is the highest of all forms, higher even than all the virtues. It is the one form that brings every other form together into a unity. Plato believed that to exist is a fundamentally good thing. Underlying all of existence, then, is the form that is pure Good-ness itself.

It is helpful to think of the Form of the Good as an originating principle giving both existence and intelligibility to all things. The Form of the Good shares its goodness with all forms and physical objects in the universe. In his famous dialogue *The Republic*, Plato describes the Form of the Good as the cause of all that is right and beautiful in the world. He views the Good as the highest object of knowledge, as well as the power that gives knowledge of everything to the human mind.

If we return to our earlier examples, each horse we see in the world participates in both the form of horse-ness and in the Form of the Good. Likewise, a human act of courage participates in both the form of courage and in the Form of the Good. It is the Form of the Good that stands behind all things, both physical and nonphysical, giving them existence, as well as intelligibility, to be known and "seen" by the human intellect.

In Book VI of *The Republic*, Plato provides a discussion of the Good:

> Now, that which imparts truth to the known and the power of knowing to the knower is what I would have you term the idea of good, and this you will deem to be the cause of science, and of truth in so far as the latter becomes the subject of knowledge; beautiful too, as are both truth and knowledge, you will be right in esteeming this other nature as more beautiful than either; and, as in the previous instance, light and sight may be truly said to be like the sun, and yet not to be the sun, so in this other sphere, science and truth may be deemed to be like the good, but not the good; the good has a place of honor yet higher.[1]

Plato emphasizes the power of the Form of the Good to enlighten our minds just as the sun gives visibility to our eyes. Without the Form of the Good sharing intelligibility with our intellects, we simply cannot know reality as it truly is.

PLATO'S GOD

When looking at Plato, it's easy to see that the rift between religion and rational thought has been around for a long time. In his public life, Plato openly professed belief in the Greek gods of the Pantheon, including the big three: Zeus, Poseidon, and Hades. He used stories from Greek mythology as regular examples in his dialogues. However, if we look deeper into his teachings to his philosophy students, he often encouraged them privately to rely on their pursuit of reason over the stories of religion.

Some believe his regular referencing of the Greek gods was a cover because of the condemnation of his teacher, Socrates. Plato was present when a jury of Athenian citizens sentenced Socrates to death by hemlock poisoning on the charges of impiety toward the gods and leading the youth of Athens into error. Because Socrates questioned the Greek gods openly in his search for truth, he upset the religious status quo and the jury sentenced him to death. Plato and other students planned to help Socrates make an escape; however, Socrates famously chose to drink the poison freely as a final act of philosophical integrity to the truth.

It is within Plato's description of the Form of the Good that we catch a glimpse into his deeper thoughts on theology and God. He may not have meant the Form of the Good to directly refer to God; still, the attributes of the Good have been used centuries after Plato's passing to describe what God might be like. With or without intending to, Plato stated a case for the reality of God that continued long past his lifetime.

The Form of the Good is both eternal and transcendent. It has always been and will always be. Because it exists apart from the physical world, it is not subject to the constraints of time. It is timeless and unchanging. It is the ultimate reality. The Form of the Good is perfect and incorruptible. It is the same yesterday, today, and forever, much like the God of monotheism would come to be described. Because it is unchanging, it has always existed, and it contains within itself its own being. It needs nothing else in order to exist.

Containing its own self-sufficient being, the Form of the Good is then the necessary being. For Plato, nothing can exist apart from it and we rely on its existence for our own existence. The Form of the Good shares its being with all other forms and physical objects by giving of itself to them.

Similarly, the Good is also necessary for our knowledge of all things. The Form of the Good is what allows our human intellect to know what each different thing is. It quite literally "in-forms" our minds with the form of whatever object we happen to be observing.

Finally, by giving existence and meaning to all the other forms, Plato's Form of the Good stands as the unifying source of all things. It is the single being from which the great diversity of different things comes together. The one that unites the many. The similarities here to the God of Judaism, Islam, and Christianity can be clearly seen. Plato's description of the Form of the Good will go on to become one of the foundational ideas used to discuss and interpret monotheistic revelation.

THE ALLEGORY OF THE CAVE

In Book VII of *The Republic*, Plato presents his now famous allegory of the cave. In it, he uses the analogies of shadows, light, and the sun to describe his world of forms in poetic detail. It provides an excellent summary of his larger philosophy as a whole. Like with all of *The Republic*, Plato wrote the cave allegory in his characteristic dialogue format. In the story we find the characters of Socrates and Glaucon, two philosophers, discussing how the Form of the Good calls us out of the darkness of ignorance and into the light of true knowledge.

(Socrates) And now, I said, let me show in a figure how far our nature is enlightened or unenlightened: Behold! human beings living in an underground den, which has a mouth open towards the light and reaching all along the den; here they have been from their childhood, and have their legs and necks chained so that they cannot move, and can only see before them, being prevented by the chains from turning round their heads. Above and behind them a fire is blazing at a distance, and between the fire and the prisoners there is a raised way; and you will see, if you look, a low wall built along the way, like the screen which marionette players have in front of them, over which they show the puppets.

(Glaucon) I see.

And do you see, I said, men passing along the wall carrying all sorts of vessels, and statues and figures of animals made of wood and stone and various materials, which appear over the wall? Some of them are talking, others silent.

You have shown me a strange image, and they are strange prisoners.

Like ourselves, I replied, and they see only their own shadows, or the shadows of one another, which the fire throws on the opposite wall of the cave?

True, he said; how could they see anything but the shadows if they were never allowed to move their heads?

And of the objects which are being carried in like manner they would only see the shadows?

Yes, he said.

And if they were able to converse with one another,

would they not suppose that they were naming what was actually before them?

Very true.

And suppose further that the prison had an echo which came from the other side, would they not be sure to fancy when one of the passers-by spoke that the voice which they heard came from the passing shadow?

No question, he replied.

To them, I said, the truth would be literally nothing but the shadows of the images.

That is certain.

And now look again and see what will naturally follow if the prisoners are released and disabused of their error. At first, when any of them is liberated and compelled suddenly to stand up and turn his neck round and walk and look towards the light, he will suffer sharp pains; the glare will distress him, and he will be unable to see the realities of which in his former state he had seen the shadows; and then conceive someone saying to him, that what he saw before was an illusion, but that now, when he is approaching nearer to being and his eye is turned towards more real existence, he has a clearer vision, what will be his reply? And you may further imagine that his instructor is pointing to the objects as they pass and requiring him to name them, will he not be perplexed? Will he not fancy that the shadows which he formerly saw are truer than the objects which are now shown to him?

Far truer.

And if he is compelled to look straight at the light,

will he not have a pain in his eyes which will make him turn away to take in the objects of vision which he can see, and which he will conceive to be in reality clearer than the things which are now being shown to him?

True, he said.

And suppose once more that he is reluctantly dragged up a steep and rugged ascent, and held fast until he's forced into the presence of the sun himself, is he not likely to be pained and irritated? When he approaches the light, his eyes will be dazzled, and he will not be able to see anything at all of what are now called realities.

Not all in a moment, he said.

He will require to grow accustomed to the sight of the upper world. And first he will see the shadows best, next the reflections of men and other objects in the water, and then the objects themselves; then he will gaze upon the light of the moon and the stars and the spangled heaven; and he will see the sky and the stars by night better than the sun or the light of the sun by day?

Certainly.

Last of all he will be able to see the sun, and not mere reflections of him in the water, but he will see him in his own proper place, and not in another; and he will contemplate him as he is.

Certainly.

He will then proceed to argue that this is he who gives the season and the years, and is the guardian of all that is in the visible world, and in a certain way the cause of all things which he and his fellows have been accustomed to behold?

Clearly, he said, he would first see the sun and then reason about him.

And when he remembered his old habitation, and the wisdom of the den and his fellow-prisoners, do you not suppose that he would felicitate himself on the change, and pity them?

Certainly, he would.

And if they were in the habit of conferring honours among themselves on those who were quickest to observe the passing shadows and to remark which of them went before, and which followed after, and which were together; and who were therefore best able to draw conclusions as to the future, do you think that he would care for such honours and glories, or envy the possessors of them? Would he not say with Homer,

Better to be the poor servant of a poor master, and to endure anything, rather than think as they do and live after their manner?

Yes, he said, I think that he would rather suffer anything than entertain these false notions and live in this miserable manner.

Imagine once more, I said, such a one coming suddenly out of the sun to be replaced in his old situation; would he not be certain to have his eyes full of darkness?

To be sure, he said.

And if there were a contest, and he had to compete in measuring the shadows with the prisoners who had never moved out of the den, while his sight was still weak, and before his eyes had become steady (and the time which would be needed to acquire this new habit of sight might be very considerable) would he not be ridiculous? Men would say of him that up he went and down he came without his eyes; and that it was better not even to think of ascending;

and if anyone tried to loose another and lead him up to the light, let them only catch the offender, and they would put him to death.

No question, he said.

This entire allegory, I said, you may now append, dear Glaucon, to the previous argument; the prison-house is the world of sight, the light of the fire is the sun, and you will not misapprehend me if you interpret the journey upwards to be the ascent of the soul into the intellectual world according to my poor belief, which, at your desire, I have expressed whether rightly or wrongly God knows. But, whether true or false, my opinion is that in the world of knowledge the idea of good appears last of all, and is seen only with an effort; and, when seen, is also inferred to be the universal author of all things beautiful and right, parent of light and of the lord of light in this visible world, and the immediate source of reason and truth in the intellectual; and that this is the power upon which he who would act rationally, either in public or private life must have his eye fixed.[2]

Plato's allegory of the cave is a story rich in symbolism as it outlines well the hierarchy of reality within the Platonic philosophical system. The prisoners' journey of ascent from shadows in the dark cave to firelight and ultimately into the direct light of the sun represents the journey of the human mind as it contemplates higher things. Plato urged his followers to think about the universal forms more and more until they spent much of their time meditating on the highest thing of all: the Form of the Good. He taught his students clearly that the forms and the knowledge of them are the keys to all things. For it is only upon reaching the last stage, that of seeing by the direct light of the sun, that the former prisoner can return to help his fellows still trapped in darkness.

While the theory of the forms is a small portion of Plato's overall body of thought, it begins for us the great conversation about what it is we can know about God using reason alone. One of Plato's major contributions to the philosophical image of God begins with the teaching that there can exist nonphysical things. This idea is hard for modern, scientific minds to accept as many people today only believe in what they can observe and measure. Still, most people would agree that virtues, like courage and humility, can be said to exist, though they are immeasurable apart from human action.

The realities of mathematics and physics are easier invisible concepts to grasp as we can measure them with our science. Philosophers and scientists have observed that we did not create the laws of physics; we discovered them. This infers they have a non-physical existence somewhere *out there* and not only in our minds. There are invisible, nonphysical realities that exist for our intellect to find, some measurable by science and some immeasurable.

A second contribution from Plato is his structured hierarchy of reality with which we can view the world. He placed physical things below and the perfection of the forms above. Within the forms, he set up a second hierarchy that begins with the forms of physical objects at the base and the higher forms of values and virtues in the middle. At the top of it all, he places the Form of the Good, uniting all things together into one.

In a world of "worse" and "better," Plato offers us a "best"—a gold standard against which we can measure everything else. This hierarchy of reality will come to be championed by some great minds and condemned by others as unnecessary dualism. Still, Plato provides us with a framework of order upon which we can build the discussion.

The third, and possibly most important, idea Plato gave to the conversation is his description of the Form of the Good. Here we find unique, God-like qualities emerging from within Greek philosophical thought. The Good is perfect and unchanging just as the God we speak of today is perfect and unchanging. The Good is the necessary existence where all things find their own existence, another quality we discover in the God of monotheism. The Good, and God, are both seen as the great unifier of all things. Both shed the light of knowledge on the human mind to know the world around them.

Finally, Plato urges those who wish to follow in the way of wisdom to spend as much time as possible in the contemplation of the highest Good. This admonishment may sound to modern ears as something of a call to prayer. If not prayer, then perhaps a call to think on the things that are above. It is as if Plato advises us to spend as much time as possible basking our minds in the light of the sun, soaking in the rays of wisdom and insight originating there.

From here, we turn our attention to the greatest of Plato's students, Aristotle. Aristotle was a genius in his own right who took issue with Plato's world of perfect forms and, in so doing, offered the world an even more compelling version of reality. Aristotle's rebuttal within the great conversation has echoed down through the centuries, influencing the world of thought to this very day.

CHAPTER 3

Aristotle's Everlasting Reply

> *"Aristotle may be regarded as the cultural barometer of Western history. Whenever his influence dominated the scene, it paved the way for one of history's brilliant eras; whenever it fell, so did mankind."*
>
> —Ayn Rand

Fable

You are staring off into space, mulling over all you just heard from the great Plato, when Sophia leans over and nudges your arm. Something is happening in the crowd; it appears Aristotle is about to contend with his teacher. This could get interesting . . . a battle of ancient wits about to ensue right before your eyes. The students watch with anticipation. Some study Plato's face for reactions, but the older philosopher only welcomes the rebuttal.

As Aristotle begins speaking, there is respect in his voice combined with noticeably strong conviction for his perspective.

Sophia translates what is being said in Greek, although you find it more difficult to follow than with Plato. Aristotle is precise and detailed with his words compared to the poetic quality of Plato's speech. Still, he lays out an argument against the master's theory of the forms while at the same time building upon Plato's framework. You begin to see the benefits of true philosophical dialogue and respect the ancients for their mastery of logical thought and candid debate. You lean in closer to Sophia and focus intently on her translation to gain as much of the Aristotelian insight as possible.

The Worthy Rival

There is something about a good rival that drives us to excel in ways we otherwise wouldn't. In his book *The Infinite Game*, Simon Sinek calls this type of person in our lives a *worthy rival*.[1] He says worthy rivals are invaluable because they give us a standard to measure ourselves and our ideas against. Simply by virtue of them being who they are and doing what they do, these people challenge us to be better and to achieve greater things than we otherwise would have attempted. Often these rivals excel in areas where we are weak. This can cause insecurities and resentments within us to bubble to the surface. Worthy rivals challenge us and drive us forward by making us uncomfortable with our status quo. While this combination can be irritating, it also acts as a catalyst in calling forth the greatness lying dormant within.

It is out of these worthy rivalries that extraordinary ideas and accomplishments often come to birth. Think of Leonardo da Vinci and Michelangelo, who painted in the same Italian cities, Mozart and Beethoven, musical prodigies just fifteen years apart in age, or Edison and Tesla, who competed to produce the best electrical system for the world. It can be argued that one of the greatest worthy rivalries in history must be the evolution of Plato's forms brought about by his student Aristotle. The ideas debated between these two minds had so much impact on the world of thought it is stunning to realize they lived at the same time and studied together in person.

The Renaissance painter Raphael captured this rivalry in his famous painting titled *The School of Athens*. The fresco adorns the Vatican Museum and was painted as a tribute to the pursuit of truth through philosophy. It depicts fifty of the greatest philosophical figures of antiquity gathered into a large Greco-Roman–style hall. Everywhere in the scene, philosophers are deep in discussion with one another, each holding an object or standing in a position that references their respective field of study. While there are many people in the scene, the painting centers on two figures clearly highlighted out from the rest, revealing their primacy within the world of ancient thought. These two who stand in the center of the painting are, of course, Plato and Aristotle.

In the painting, Plato is depicted as an older man with a white beard pointing up toward the sky. He looks upward while speaking to Aristotle. Aristotle, standing next to him, is portrayed as a younger man in the prime of life whose face looks to Plato. He is shown extending the palm of his hand down toward the earth. Raphael's work is as intellectually intriguing as it is visually stunning.

The painter left no commentary on the work and gave history no reason why he chose to represent each philosopher the way he did. Something of a consensus has emerged over time as an accepted interpretation of his meaning, especially regarding these two central figures. The interpretation says that Raphael was painting the great divergence of thought between the two schools of Platonism and Aristotelianism. In the painting, Aristotle stands ever so slightly in front of Plato, he appears slightly taller, and the crowd gathered appears to look a bit more in Aristotle's direction. This primacy of attention in the work translates to the new primacy of Aristotelian thought over that of Plato's.

Plato is shown pointing up toward his ideal world of forms, where the purest knowledge is found. Aristotle is shown directing us down in a fundamental rejection of Plato's ideal world. Aristotle's main divergence from Plato's thought looked like this: He took the two Platonic worlds, the one of physical objects and the one of ideal forms, combined them together, and placed them both within the context of physical objects alone. In other words, for Aristotle, the world of forms does not exist on its own. He believed the forms do exist, but only within individual, real things and not apart on their own, floating around in some ideal realm. Aristotle emphasized strongly that philosophy should remain grounded in the observable world.

Aristotle's palm is pointing down because, for him, the world around us is the only place where true knowledge can be found. The similarity between Aristotle and scientists of today is an interesting one. Plato spent his time contemplating the intelligible world and shunning the physical one. Aristotle taught his students, instead, to intently study the physical world in order to arrive at truth from the ground up. Within the plant itself, within the horse itself, and within the human being itself is where you will find the world of matter and Plato's world of forms combined.

ARISTOTLE'S LIFE

Aristotle was born in the city of Stagira in northern Greece (then Macedonia) around the year 384 BC. The name Aristotle meant something like "superior," or "the best purpose," perhaps a prophecy for what the young man would later become. His father was royal physician to King Philip II of Macedon, but died when Aristotle was still young, leaving the boy to be raised by a family guardian. He was well educated throughout childhood and, at the age of seventeen, was sent to study philosophy under Plato at the Academy of Athens. There he stayed for twenty years, learning diligently from his mentor until Plato's death in 347 BC. Aristotle left the academy soon after, likely over disagreements with the new leadership of the school.

After leaving Plato's academy, Aristotle spent some solitary time on the island of Lesbos, where he studied zoology and botany much like Charles Darwin would two millennia later on the Galapagos Islands. While on Lesbos, Aristotle theorized that all living things must have originated from the sea. He observed the abundance of marine life and the wide variety of species found in the ocean. From these observations, he concluded that the sea must have been the primary source of all life, and that land-dwelling organisms were derived from marine ancestors.

On the island of Lesbos, Aristotle married Pythias and the couple gave birth to a daughter of the same name. Aristotle left his island life in 343 BC when he was summoned by the king of Macedon to become the head of the royal academy there. In Macedon, he would spend his time tutoring three students who would all later grow up to be kings, the most notable of which was Alexander the Great.

In a final career move, Aristotle returned to Athens to found his own school of philosophy known as the Lyceum. Aristotle and his Lyceum students were referred to as *peripatetics*, meaning "to walk around," thanks to their habit of wandering about the beautiful covered walkways during lectures. The historian Will Durant notes that Aristotle wrote twenty-seven philosophical dialogues, like those of Plato; however, all of them were lost during the barbarian invasion of Rome.[2] The copious amount of his teachings we have today were likely his lecture notes or the notes taken down by his more diligent students.

Aristotle taught a massive volume of work during his lifetime spanning every subject imaginable. His prolific teachings are the reason he would later become so influential in many different fields of study, including metaphysics, logic, politics, ethics, psychology, and biology. He is widely regarded as one of the most—if not *the* most—significant thinker to shape Western thought. One theory in particular is important for our exploration of Aristotle's contribution to the great conversation: the four causes.

ARISTOTLE'S FOUR CAUSES

Aristotle believed all physical things exist thanks to four causes—the first two of which are *matter* and *form*, or the material cause and the formal cause. The other two causes are the *efficient cause* and the *final cause*, which we will delve into sequentially. For Aristotle, everything that exists in the universe is made up from these four causes, which he details in Book V of his *Metaphysics*.

Let's use the examples of a wooden table (an inanimate object), a horse (a living creature), and the virtue of courage (a nonphysical reality) to help illustrate how each of the four causes operates within the Aristotelian system. The material cause is simply what a thing is made of. The specific wording from Book V of Aristotle's *Metaphysics* is "that out of which" something is made.[3] In our first example of the wooden table, the material cause is the wood. For our horse example, the material would be the animal's flesh and bone. In our example of the virtue of courage, the material cause is the human action taking place, for example, protesting in front of city hall for a cause one believes in. The material cause is straightforward and easy to comprehend; it is simply the matter out of which a thing is made.

The second cause for Aristotle is the formal cause. The formal cause he defines as "the account of what it is to be." It reveals into what arrangement the matter is configured. This is where we see Aristotle continuing the thought of his predecessor Plato. With the formal cause, he takes Plato's forms out of the sky and places them within each individual thing. Aristotle agrees that the forms of things do exist, but for him they exist only within the thing itself. Applied to our examples, the material of wood is arranged into the form of a table, the horse's flesh and bone are arranged into the form of a horse, and the courageous human action is arranged into the form of a protest. The formal cause for Aristotle is what gives intelligible meaning to the material out of which the thing is made.

The third of the four causes Aristotle names the efficient cause. The efficient cause is described as "the primary source of change or rest." This cause aims to explain who or what is causing the thing to happen. It provides an explanation for who made it, or what caused it to come into being. In our three examples, the wooden table is constructed by the carpenter and the horse is brought into being by its parents. For the virtue of courage, the efficient cause is the human being performing the action.

Lastly, we have what Aristotle calls the final cause. This cause is defined as "the end, that for the sake of which a thing is done." It can be thought of as the "why" behind something's existence, the reason for which it is. In our examples, the wooden table is made for the sake of having a meal on its tabletop. For natural objects, such as our horse, the final cause is to grow from a pony into an adult horse and do proper horse things. In the example of the courageous act, the final cause is to bring about meaningful change. By protesting an injustice, the courageous human attempts to change his or her world for the better.

Aristotle believed the final cause acted on things differently than did the other three causes. He taught that the final cause puts things into motion by activating their internal desire to reach their ideal state. He writes, "The final cause, then, produces motion as being loved, but all other things move by being moved."[4] In some ways, the distinction might be compared to internal and external motivation. The final cause acts as a powerful internal motivation that helps things reach their intended purpose.

EVERYTHING HAS A TELOS

The idea that there is a purpose for everything and a reason toward which each thing is moving brings us to another of Aristotle's concepts. He introduced the Greek term *telos* as a way to describe a thing's purpose, intent, or goal. For Aristotle, the telos of a thing is the end toward which it is heading and the ideal state a thing is trying to achieve. In his mind, everything has an inherent purpose and "final end," even inanimate objects. In this way, the telos is directly tied to a thing's final cause.

For example, the telos of an acorn is to become a fully grown oak tree that bears leaves and more acorns. The telos of our pony is to become an adult horse that does horse things and has more ponies. The telos of a child is to become a well-rounded, fully functioning, virtuous adult who contributes to society in a meaningful way and who also produces more humans.

The telos helps to explain the meaning behind why a thing exists and why it undergoes change the way it does. It also helps us understand whether a thing is changing, or moving, in the *right* direction and so helps us evaluate if a thing is becoming more or less excellent according to its nature. Is the tree withering and dying or is it growing and flourishing? Is the human person becoming more corrupt in their daily actions or are they growing more virtuous each day?

To understand this change in a thing, Aristotle often used the two concepts of potentiality and actuality within his philosophical system in regard to telos. These words are still used today in the terms *potential* and *actual*. The idea is that things have a certain potential to become what they are intended to be. They begin with the potential to fulfill their specific purpose, or telos, and over time they either actualize that potential or fail to do so. The acorn has the potential to become an oak tree, but that doesn't necessarily mean it will ever get there. As the acorn grows into a tree, Aristotle says it is both actualizing its potential and fulfilling its telos at the same time.

THE PROBLEM OF CHANGE

One of Aristotle's main curiosities in life was the question of why things undergo change the way they do. He asked questions like, "Why do things go from the state of having potential to a state of actualizing it?" and "Why is there any movement or change at all in the world?" We can see this thought process clearly in his definition of time, which he simply calls "a measure of change."[5] All things undergo change, but why? His four causes helped Aristotle answer that question for individual things, but he wanted to go bigger—all the way back to the beginning of it all. What could have started all this movement and change in the universe in the first place?

In Aristotle's time, and for centuries after him, scholars assumed the void of space was static and eternal. The universe had always just been there, without a beginning in time, so they did not see the need to explain its existence; it was what it was and always had been. In Aristotle's inquiry on the beginning of all change, he was specifically concerned with what caused the first movement of the stars and celestial bodies in their orbits. Space was static, but all the movement and change occurring within it fascinated him.

Aristotle used logic to argue there simply had to be something that started all the motion and change we see in the world. This argument we now refer to as the problem of *infinite regression*. Simply put, it says you cannot have an infinitely long line of dominoes without something or someone there to push over the first one. Because everything depends on something else to bring it into being or set it into motion, change cannot go back indefinitely without something that's unchanging there to start it out. In other words, in the chain of cause and effect, there must exist a First Cause.

Aristotle's answer to this ultimate problem of infinite regression is where we catch a glimpse into his ideas on God. Like Plato, Aristotle publicly subscribed to the gods of the Greek pantheon. Within his philosophical system, however, his students saw something different. His ideas on what divine things were like did not match up with the common descriptions of Zeus or Athena. As with Plato, the world would see in Aristotle's teachings some divine attributes similar to those professed by Judaism, Islam, and Christianity.

Aristotle's Unmoved Mover

Aristotle introduces the Unmoved Mover as his explanation for the origin of movement and change in the universe. The Unmoved Mover, also known as the Prime Mover or First Cause, is a divine being who exists in the heavens, a nonphysical place out among the stars. The Unmoved Mover transcends the physical world while still maintaining an effect on it.

Aristotle describes his Unmoved Mover as immutable, meaning it does not undergo change in any way. Since Aristotle believed time is a measure of change, he argued that the Unmoved Mover must necessarily exist outside of time and separate from it altogether. The Unmoved Mover must be unaffected by the passing of time; otherwise, it would be just one more link in the chain of motion and change. In fact, movement *is* change for Aristotle. Movement is the actuality of potentiality, or a change in something's state. For example, a horse moves from one place to another, or an acorn changes from a lower state to a higher one by growing into a tree. Thus, by naming this being the Unmoved Mover, Aristotle recognizes it must not move or change in any way like horses or acorns do.

Importantly for Aristotle, if something is subject to change, then it is imperfect; it still requires some type of transformation to actualize its full potential. Since the Unmoved Mover is not subject to change, this means it must necessarily be an already perfect being, completely actualized and containing no potential. This being does not go from a state of having potential to actualizing it. Rather, the Unmoved Mover always exists in a permanent state of full actualization. There is nothing more for it to become; it is already perfect in every way.

Because of this state of pure actuality, the Unmoved Mover is the only being in the universe capable of initiating movement and change without itself being acted upon by any outside force. The Unmoved Mover is the one who pushes over the first domino in the long, endless chain of movement throughout time. For Aristotle, the Unmoved Mover is the necessary existence required to explain all change in the universe. Without this being, no motion would be possible.

A fascinating question arises here. How is it that a being who does not move or change can cause other things to move and change? How does the Unmoved Mover *push* over the first domino without performing any act of *pushing*? Aristotle's answer to this question displays his genius and depth of thought. The solution he offers is rooted in his concept of the final cause from his four causes theory. He argues that the Unmoved Mover is so perfect and so desirable that it causes all the universe to move and change out of *desire*. The Unmoved Mover draws all things toward itself simply by being who it is.

Through a creative twist of thought, Aristotle introduces a method of acting on the world without the actor having to do anything at all. The Unmoved Mover becomes both the first cause and the final cause of everything in the universe. All things desire to be closer to it and to be more like it in every way. Physical things move to actualize their potential to more closely imitate the Unmoved Mover, who is pure and perfect actuality.

Aristotle believed the Unmoved Mover existed somewhere beyond the furthest stars, in a world of pure rational thought and no physical dimensions. In other words, it is transcendent; it exists apart from and beyond the normal physical world. In *On the Heavens*, Aristotle writes, "It is clear then that there is neither place, nor void, nor time, outside of heaven . . . . Hence whatever is true, is of such a nature as not to occupy any place, nor does time age it; nor is there any change in any of the things which lie beyond the outermost motion; they continue through their entire duration unalterable and unmodified, living the best and most self-sufficient lives."[6] Notice here he seems to be teaching the existence of multiple Unmoved Movers as compared to a singular Mover; however, consensus believes the singular Mover was where his thought ended up.

For Aristotle, the Unmoved Mover is a detached divine being who is not intimately involved with the day-to-day happenings of the material world. It may cause the change in the world, but it doesn't seem to care about the world it changes. Aristotle's Mover does not do things like speak, move around, or intervene in human history, as these would all require movement. The Unmoved Mover, like the void of space in Aristotle's time, has always just been there.

So, what is this Mover doing all day long? If it exists in the world of pure rational thought and does not perform any actions, does it do anything or is it just existing there for us to admire? To answer this, Aristotle deduced that the Unmoved Mover is perfect and must therefore be engaged in the highest rational activity: contemplation. The only problem now is that there is nothing better than the Unmoved Mover for it to think about. Aristotle ultimately concludes that the Unmoved Mover must be engaged in the most perfect of all contemplation: self-contemplation. In other words, the Unmoved Mover is perfect rational thought thinking about itself.

The Aristotelian roots run deep in monotheistic theology, especially within the ideas of Western Christianity. Christian theologians in the centuries that follow will use this idea of the Unmoved Mover's self-contemplation to help explain the Trinitarian God. Instead of one being eternally thinking about itself, the Holy Trinity becomes one God in three persons eternally contemplating one another. From the Unmoved Mover giving movement to all things, God is the Creator of all things. As the cosmos mirrors the Unmoved Mover, we'll see creation reflecting its Creator. An ordered being creates an ordered universe, which Aristotle explains in the form of a ladder or chain.

THE LADDER OF NATURE

From Aristotle's keen observations of the natural world, he noticed life appears to be arranged into a ladder of increasing complexity. He called this concept the Ladder of Nature and taught that things are ordered from the simplest life to the more complex. As one moves along the ladder, one approaches nearer to the divine.

In one of his seminal works, *De Anima*, or "On the Soul," Aristotle taught the Ladder of Nature in detail. An important note here is that the term *soul*, for Aristotle, is more of an animating principle than it is the immortal soul of religion. Specifically, he uses the Greek word *psyche* as a way of explaining the inherent powers or abilities of living things. As we will see, Aristotle assigned a type of soul, or animating principle, to all living things.

Another important note is that the living things on each subsequent higher rung of the ladder have their own unique abilities plus all the abilities of the levels below them. The second rung has its own unique powers plus those of the first rung. The fourth rung contains its own powers plus those of the third, second, and first rungs, and so on. As we ascend Aristotle's Ladder of Nature, we grow in proximity to the divine, but we do not lose any of the abilities of the rungs below.

The first rung of the ladder begins with inanimate, physical objects. This level includes things like rocks or basic minerals. These objects are composed of physical material and form, but they do not possess an animating soul and therefore do not grow, move, sense, or change of their own accord. This is the only rung of the ladder that does not possess an animating principle.

On the second rung of the Ladder of Nature, we find plant life. As with the first rung, this level possesses physical material, as well as form; however, here we see a new power—what Aristotle calls a nutritive or vegetative soul. Plants possess the ability to grow, feed, and reproduce and it is the vegetative soul that empowers each plant with these abilities.

The third rung of the ladder is composed of the animal kingdom. Here we have what Aristotle calls the sensitive soul empowering animals with a host of new abilities. Animals can sense the world around them and react to it accordingly. They have the ability of perception and minimal cognition, as well as movement of their own accord. The sensitive soul empowers the instinctual behaviors of animals and provides for their migration from place to place. In keeping with the lower rungs, animals also possess all the powers of the vegetative soul and the matter and form of the first rung.

On the fourth rung of the Ladder of Nature we find ourselves. Human beings are empowered with a special power all their own, one that brings them closer to the divine and separates them out from the other animals. Humans have what Aristotle calls the rational or intellective soul. We have the unique abilities of engaging in reasoning, moral deliberation, and abstract thought. These abilities are what Aristotle considers the highest and most noble functions of all the souls. We can formulate ideas and reflect on concepts far beyond the immediate sensory experience of other animals. Humans make decisions based on a moral code, right versus wrong, and act with or against virtue.

The fifth and final rung of the ladder holds Aristotle's celestial spheres. Based on his observations and understanding of the cosmos in his day, he believed there existed multiple, transparent spheres around the earth that made up the heavens—think here of something like transparent Russian stacking dolls in the shape of spheres. The earth was thought to be the center of the ancient universe and these subsequently larger spheres circled the earth, extending out into deep space. The sun was fixed to one sphere, the planets to another, the outer stars to a third, and so on. The celestial spheres rotate in set directions like an eternal carousel. As they move, the stars and planets fixed to them move also. This is how Aristotle and many ancient astronomers accounted for the movement of the stars and planets in the nighttime sky.

The celestial spheres were not made of earthly elements such as air, fire, earth, and water. Aristotle taught that the spheres occupied the highest rung on the Ladder of Nature and were the closest things to the divine Unmoved Mover who was the ultimate cause of their movements. Due to this proximity, they were made of a fifth element he named *aether*. This material was perfect, unchanging, and transparent, something of a hybrid between the physical and divine worlds.

ARISTOTLE'S LASTING INFLUENCE

Aristotle was a mind of unbelievable genius. If Plato gave us a framework with which to view reality, then Aristotle gave us his own revised version of that framework. More than that, Aristotle gave us specific language with which to discuss these challenging concepts surrounding the nature of reality and the divine attributes. In a time when scientific research was limited, he emphasized the need for strict observation and classification of nature. By doing this he became one of the main precursors to the modern scientific approach. What we have covered here is but a very small portion of Aristotle's overall body of work. His discussions in the fields of logic, politics, and ethics were equally influential to the growth and development of their respective fields.

Aristotle believed in an ordered universe that underwent observable change. Things seem inherently driven to achieve a specific end: a telos, a potential within that's waiting to be actualized. He saw this everywhere, from the furthest cosmos to the closest plants and animals, even to human beings as we desire to grow and develop our character in order to become more actualized people.

The great philosopher influenced the development of theology based on his Ladder of Nature and his description of the Unmoved Mover. He likely had no idea just how strong his influence on future monotheistic religion would be, just as many of us today have little idea just how big an impact he's had on the descriptions of God we grew up with.

Aristotle gave us a logical basis upon which to base our ideas of God. The Unmoved Mover, out of necessity, must stand outside of time and change. For the problem of infinite regression to be solved, there must be a First Cause, who is itself unmoved. This being cannot be physical in nature since all physical things undergo movement and change. It must be a being that is fully actualized, containing zero potential. Every possibility already actualized, nothing greater for it to become at any time—a being already perfect in nature. A being so perfect and desirable that all things move in a continual procession toward it. So perfect, in fact, that the only worthy activity of such a being is the continual contemplation of itself.

Aristotle's views on the divine nature and on the nature of the world were highly regarded and spread throughout Greece during his lifetime and beyond his death in 322 BC. He was an important teacher to philosophers, politicians, and kings alike. It was one of his pupils, however, who would help spread Aristotle's teachings far beyond Greece and throughout the ancient Western world. His most famous of students, Alexander the Great, would take Aristotelian philosophy on a worldwide tour as he conquered lands and spread Greek culture all along the way.

CHAPTER 4

The Synthesis of Faith and Reason

"What has Athens to do with Jerusalem?"

—Tertullian

Fable

As Aristotle completes his presentation, the mob of eager students surrounds the two masters, asking questions and debating specific points to offer insights of their own. You look down at the ground for a moment, lost in the ideas, then glance over to your friend who sits quietly by, waiting for you to emerge from thought.

After a few moments, you speak. "That was . . . quite impressive; I think I understood about ten percent of what he said. These guys have obviously spent a lot of time thinking about the world, but even I can see where they are wrong on some major points."

"Yes," Sophia replies. "The knowledge you have from modern

science makes it easier to see the mistakes and errors. No philosopher has ever gotten it all right. The search for wisdom is just that, a search, and often a difficult one. The search is worthwhile, however, as the treasure discovered lasts forever. Those ideas you just heard will enlighten untold billions of people for centuries to come."

"How is that even possible?"

Her voice calm with a hint of excitement, Sophia says, "Close your eyes, take my hand, and I will show you."

Your adrenaline races again as you wait for what's in store. You grab Sophia's hand and close your eyes tightly in anticipation. A few seconds later you hear her say, "Now open."

You open your eyes to see a city skyline filled with both ancient and modern structures spread out before you. The two of you are sitting in another garden area on top of a hillside this time, about half a mile from the city.

"Welcome to Jerusalem, also known as the Holy City," Sophia says, then adds, "present day."

As you look out over Jerusalem, your gaze is drawn to two massive domes, one silver and one gold, standing out amid the surroundings. There are high bell towers, some smaller domes, and cathedral spires rising out of the skyline in other places. Modern office buildings lie farther off in the distance, serving as a contrasting backdrop to the ancient architecture in the foreground. On the hillside just below you sits an aboveground cemetery with hundreds of raised, stone burial chambers spread out over a portion of the hill. You look around for a while and take it all in.

After a moment, Sophia begins a guided tour. "We are standing on the Mount of Olives, overlooking the Old City of Jerusalem.

The garden of Gethsemane, where Jesus of Nazareth came to pray the night before his crucifixion, is located at the base of this hill. The graves you see below us hold the remains of some of the most influential Jewish people in history, including prophets and kings. This site has been used as a burial ground for a very long time, spanning back over three thousand years. It is a sacred place for Judaism, Islam, and Christianity—a place pilgrims come to visit from all over the world."

Pointing out toward the city, Sophia asks, "Do you see the two large domes there in the center?"

"Yes," you reply.

"The silver dome sits atop the Church of the Holy Sepulchre, a building that contains two of the holiest sites in Christianity. Tradition teaches that is the place where Jesus was crucified on Calvary and where he rose again from the tomb."

Fascinating, you think to yourself.

"Now look to the large, golden dome just to the right. That is known as the Dome of the Rock. Within its walls, you will find some of the most sacred sites for Islam and Judaism."

"For two different faiths? In the same building?"

"Yes, it is sacred for Christians as well. The Dome of the Rock covers something called the Foundation Stone. Jewish tradition holds that this massive rock is the site where God called forth the creation of the world.

"In Islamic tradition, the Foundation Stone is the place where the Prophet Muhammad began his night journey from Earth into Heaven. The Qur'an describes this miracle as a sacred journey where Muhammad spoke with Allah face-to-face. He was taken up during the span of one night and was brought back down to Earth seven hundred miles away in the city of Mecca. Muslims believe the Foundation Stone will also be the place where the trumpet will sound on the final day. As you can see, this one site holds great significance for many people."

You take a few moments to soak in the history all around you. So many wars have been fought over this very small expanse of ground and now you begin to realize why it could be such a place of contention. Billions of people have devoted their lives to the teachings of these three major world faiths. It is at the same time fascinating and sad that there is so much conflict in a city so sacred.

You turn to Sophia and ask, "So, why did we leave Athens to come to Jerusalem? What's the connection? What do Plato and Aristotle have to do with religion?"

"I'm glad you asked."

Alexander's Hellenization

The impact of Plato and Aristotle's philosophies, along with Greek culture in general, is immeasurably large. Nearly every culture introduced to their ideas absorbed them in some way, often melding their native cultures into some form of a Greek hybrid. The spread of Greek ideas was due mainly to the quality of the ideas themselves. The philosophy was genius, yet practical, and the introduction of Greek institutions served the common good. Word of mouth naturally spread these ideas throughout surrounding lands and beyond. But there was another reason for the widespread dissemination of Greek culture into much of the known world at the time. This reason stemmed from the ambitions of Aristotle's student, Alexander the Great, and his desire to conquer Persia and then the world.

Alexander of Macedon, or Alexander the Great, is famous for his ten-year military crusade from his home country of Macedon in northern Greece all the way to the Middle East and western Asia, spanning northeastern Africa all the way to parts of India. It is said that the young king was enamored of Homer's epics and thanks to the influence of his tutor, Aristotle, he often carried with him a gifted copy of Homer while on military campaign.

Let's be clear, Alexander's conquests left tremendous destruction and loss of life in their wake. More than twenty cities were conquered, mostly destroyed, and then rebuilt and renamed in Alexander's honor, the most famous of which is modern-day Alexandria in Egypt. Apart from leaving behind his namesake, a secondary result of such a vast conquest of land was the exposure of numerous and diverse peoples to Greek culture. Some speculate that Alexander's great hope was for the unification of the world under one banner. He was not alone in his belief that Greece held the highest of cultural ideals. In fact, the vision of a world united under Greek customs was lauded by a number of classical thinkers.

With Alexander's death in 323 BC, the spread of Greek ideas and customs throughout the world increased—a period known as Hellenization, because the Greeks were thought to have descended from Hellen, grandson of Prometheus. The spread of Greek culture was so successful because the conquerors allowed native cultures to remain in place. Instead of forcing 100 percent adoption of Greek ideas, they encouraged a combination (or syncretism) of Greek life with native life. Later in history, the Roman, Christian, and British Empires would adopt similar strategies to great success.

During the period of Hellenization, the newly introduced Greek language, culture, myths, educational system, and philosophies melded with each culture they encountered. Before his death, Alexander had built gymnasiums as social centers of his new cities and went so far as to encourage intermarriage between native peoples and Greeks, a practice rarely promoted before this time. He even allowed natives to join his armies and fight alongside Greek soldiers. This display of trust and cultural support served to spread the effects of Hellenization deep within each new place it encountered.

One remarkable vestige of Hellenization was the great Musaeum of Alexandria. The Musaeum, which translates to "the Institution of the Muses," was one of the world's first research centers dedicated solely to the collection and study of the arts, sciences, and intellectual pursuits. The muses in Greek mythology were goddesses who inspired humanity toward literature, science, art, poetry, music, and myth. As you can tell, this is where our modern concept of museums arose and where the phrase "to muse" on a piece of art originates.

The Musaeum of Alexandria became a unique collection of knowledge from all over the world. Intellectuals traveled from far and wide to study there, bringing with them outside learnings from various cultures and intellectual traditions. Famous minds studied there, including Euclid, the founder of geometry; Dionysius Thrax, the inventor of grammatical structure; Herophilus, the founder of anatomy studies; and Archimedes, the famous astronomer, scientist, and inventor. It is likely that sections of the Old Testament Scriptures, including the Song of Songs, were written there as well.

The Great Library of Alexandria, housed within the Musaeum, grew to be one of the largest collections of papyrus scrolls in all of ancient history. Because the library was not associated with any particular school, there occurred a great mixing of knowledge among its scholars and a freedom to pursue truth in any of its forms. At the height of its influence, the Library of Alexandria was reported to have had between four hundred thousand and seven hundred thousand papyrus scrolls within its walls,[1] representing the greatest single storehouse of knowledge in the known world.

This collection of knowledge helped spread the ideas of Plato and Aristotle ever further, eventually leading to one of the most profound and lasting impacts of all—their tremendous influence on religion. It is difficult to separate out just how big an impact Greek philosophy has had on the world of faith, as the two are now forever intertwined within modern belief systems and creeds.

The Synthesizers

Plato and Aristotle used reasoned debate to tease out attributes of the divine. They likely did not have access to the ancient texts of the Hebrew Scriptures and they lived long before the Bible or the Qur'an would be assembled and disseminated. Their discovery of God via philosophy and reason can be likened to a difficult climb up a very high mountain. It is arduous, if not impossibly hard work and often slow going. There will be many mistakes made along the way and, if the truth is ever found, there is almost no way to prove it to others.

Revelations of faith, on the other hand, what we receive from religion, can be likened to rays of light shining down from Heaven on the same high mountaintop. Revelation here refers to the holy texts and words of the prophets—things like the Torah, the Bible, and the Qur'an, which are believed to have come to humanity directly from the divine source. Philosophy digs through the mud to find some level of clarity about the divine while revelation is given to us by God already whole and complete.

With these two forms of knowledge in mind, we arrive at the great synthesizers of history. This group of scholars existed within their respective worlds of faith as people deeply devoted to the truth of revelation, as well as to the truths of philosophy. They spent their lives on the mountaintop, searching for deeper understanding in whatever form they could find it. The synthesizers were often ostracized by their devout peers for reading pagan texts like Plato's dialogues and Aristotle's *Metaphysics*. The divide between faith and reason existed in their day just as it does now, but that did not deter them from searching for truth. We are now the recipients of their brave contributions toward bridging the gap between faith and reason.

Due to the constraints of space, we will narrow our focus to two of the most influential synthesizers from each monotheistic faith: Philo of Alexandria and Moses Maimonides representing Judaism, Ibn Sina (Avicenna) and Ibn Rush'd (Averroes) from Islam, and Augustine of Hippo and Thomas Aquinas as representatives of Christianity. Each of these six scholars spent their lives "camping out" on the mountaintop. They welcomed the truth they found in Plato's and Aristotle's long ascent up the mountain and they bathed their faces in the light of revelation as it shined down on them from above. They set themselves to the challenging task of combining philosophy and revelation into one cohesive whole and they did not let go of either side no matter how high the cost.

JUDAISM

Philo of Alexandria (20 BC–50 AD)

Philo lived in the city named after Alexander the Great around the end of the first century BC and into the middle of the first century AD. He was one of the first known synthesizers to continue the conversation of Plato and Aristotle within the context of the Jewish faith. Little is known about his life other than he was born into a prominent family and was educated within the Greek schooling system as part of a Hellenistic Jewish community in Alexandria, Egypt.

As a devout Jew, Philo wrote extensive commentary on the Hebrew Scriptures, as well as essays on Greek philosophy and contemporary topics of his day. One of the most important techniques Philo used to bring together Greek philosophy with Judaism was his explanation that many of the stories in the first five books of the Jewish Torah, known as the Pentateuch, were to be taken allegorically or metaphorically and not literally. This interpretation was later taken up by most of the other synthesizers and has become the traditional starting point to bring faith and reason together. The literal versus metaphorical interpretation of scriptural stories is a debate that rages on today; however, Philo insisted the metaphorical side must win out if there is ever to be a rational understanding of God. He argued that philosophy's description of the divine attributes explained the nature of God in ways the anthropomorphic stories of Scripture did not.

A second major contribution of Philo was his theological development of the Greek term *Logos*, which carries with it a rich and complex meaning not easily translated into modern English. The term Logos means something like "an originating principle of order or knowledge." Logos is also often interpreted as "word," "reason," or "plan." It can be thought of as the deeper meaning behind the words.

For an example of Logos, try to think of a time you attempted to explain an idea but were at a loss for words. The words in themselves are the sounds we use to communicate our ideas and intended meaning. You may not have been able to conjure up accurate words at the time, but what you meant to say was still within you. It is this deeper meaning within that could be considered your Logos. The words, whether you found them or not, were simply tools to communicate the deeper meaning.

Another example of the Greek idea for Logos can be found in our modern-day use of the same word. We are all familiar with company logos, or symbols used to identify a brand. When marketing teams the world over get together to design their company's logo, the conversation often goes something like this:

"What is the deeper meaning about our company or product we want to convey to our customers when they see our logo?"

"What ethos do we want our company to carry and how do we design that into a simple, graphical representation?"

The greatest achievement of marketing is to design a logo that transmits meaning so powerfully the company becomes permanently embedded deep within our minds and culture.

Philo believed strongly in Platonic philosophy as well as Judaism, which led him to replace Plato's Form of the Good with Yahweh. He then offered the idea that the Divine Logos was the Wisdom of God and described it as a secondary, lesser divine being, sitting just below God on the hierarchy of nature. Per the Greek rules of philosophy, the highest being had to be perfectly unchanging. Philo used the idea of Logos as a divine intermediary tasked with creating the world and performing God's desired actions in it. The Logos possessed many of the attributes of God but was secondary to Him and therefore free to change and act without God having to do so. This thought process allowed Philo's God to fulfill the laws of philosophy while also allowing his Logos to perform the religious stories of the Torah.

The concept of the Logos greatly influenced Jewish theology and, later, Christianity. The historian Will Durant notes, "In the twenty-fourth chapter of Ecclesiasticus we are told that 'Wisdom is the first product of God, created from the beginning of the world.' Here and in the first chapter of Proverbs are the earliest Hebrew forms of the doctrine of the Logos."[2]

Christianity would later claim Philo's Logos as the precursor to the theology of Jesus as the incarnate "Word" of God. Where the Logos was God's wisdom personified in Judaism, it now becomes equal in nature to God as the second person of the Holy Trinity. This development of Philo's Logos theology can be clearly seen in the first chapter of John's Gospel:

> In the beginning was the Word [Logos], and the Word was with God, and the Word was God. He was with God in the beginning. Through him all things were made; without him nothing was made that has been made.[3]

Here we see the Gospel of John using the Greek word Logos in direct reference to the second person of the Trinity, Jesus Christ, who is named in verse seventeen of the same chapter.

What John does here by referencing Christ with the concept of Logos is help readers connect the person of Jesus to the Divine Word, the incarnate "statement, argument, reason" of God. Christ is God's mind made manifest. Christian theology views Jesus as the second person of the Trinity who is one with God and not a secondary created being like Philo's Wisdom.

Philo's third contribution to the great discussion was his development of Plato's world of forms. He preferred Plato's version of Greek philosophy and so worked to combine the world of forms with his world of faith. In defense of Plato, Philo proclaimed that the unseen world of forms does indeed exist as the ideas of created things within the mind of God. The ideal forms for Philo are the perfect, creative ideas of God. This concept stuck with theologians for centuries and continued to develop within the worlds of Judaism, Islam, Christianity, and beyond.

Moses Maimonides (1138–1204 AD)

The second great synthesizer of Greek philosophy and Judaism was Moses ben Maimon, or Moses Maimonides in the West. To get an idea of just how influential Maimonides was to the whole of Jewish tradition, one may simply read the epitaph written on his gravestone in Tiberias, near the Sea of Galilee. It reads, "From Moses to Moses, there was no one like Moses." His grave remains one of the most visited pilgrimage sites in the Jewish tradition.

Moses Maimonides was born in Córdoba, Spain, in 1138 but was forced to flee with his family to Egypt at a young age due to persecution from the new fundamentalist Islamic regime who gained control of the region. Maimonides is most known for his comprehensive, fourteen-volume work titled the Mishneh Torah. This extensive manuscript was the first ever to codify and condense the entirety of Jewish oral tradition and Jewish law into one place. It was the opus of his life and became a permanent, foundational text in the world of Judaism. Maimonides hoped that once a Jewish scholar mastered the Torah, the only other textbook he would ever need was his Mishneh Torah. For many scholars, this turned out to be exactly the case.

There are thirteen articles of faith within Judaism representing its foundations. Devout Jews recite these thirteen articles each day in the synagogue using their poetic form known as the Ani Maamin or "I believe." The thirteen tenets of belief were written by Moses Maimonides to summarize what is most important to the faith. The first four are relevant for the synthesis of Greek ideas.

The First Four of the Thirteen Articles of Faith[4]

1. The first principle: The belief in the existence of the Creator; that is, the belief that there exists a Being who requires no other cause for His existence, but is Himself the cause of all beings.

2. The second principle: The belief in the unity of God; that is, the belief that the Being who is the cause of everything in existence is One, not like the unity of a group or class, composed of a certain number of individuals, or the unity of one simple thing that is divisible *ad infinitum*, but as a unity the like of which does not exist.

3. The third principle: The belief in the incorporeality of God; that is, the belief that this One Creator has neither bodily form nor substance, that He is not a force contained in a body, and that no corporeal quality or action can be attributed to Him.

4. The fourth principle: The belief in the eternity of God; that is, the belief that God alone is without a beginning, while no other being is without a beginning.

In these first four principles concerning the nature of God, we find the influence of the Greek philosophers on Judaism. The first tenet parallels Plato and Aristotle's belief that the Form of the Good and the Unmoved Mover, respectively, must be uncaused so as to be the origin of all caused things.

The second tenet describes the unity of God, saying, "A unity the like of which does not exist." While Maimonides was influenced by many Jewish scholars, we find here hints of Plato's Form of the Good and Aristotle's Unmoved Mover in that both are indivisible. The third tenet, which says, "No corporeal quality can be attributed to Him," speaks to the fact that God cannot be made up of matter; physicality simply cannot explain what He is. He transcends matter and thus the world of the senses.

In the fourth tenet we have God's eternity, another belief commonly held by most monotheistic religions. In the Form of the Good and the Unmoved Mover, Greek philosophy gave Judaism the rational means to explain why God must necessarily exist outside of both time and change—therefore being eternal in nature. Here we see that concept fully woven into Jewish belief.

Maimonides wrote a second book, another opus of sorts, where he more explicitly carried on the great conversation of Plato and Aristotle. *The Guide for the Perplexed*, later referred to simply as *The Guide*, is an attempt to reconcile Aristotelianism with Jewish theology. In Maimonides's own words, *The Guide*'s purpose was "to enlighten a religious man who has been trained to believe in the truth of our holy Law, who conscientiously fulfills his moral and religious duties, and at the same time has been successful in his philosophical studies."[5] It is important to note Maimonides taught that *The Guide* was not for everyone. Rather, it was written only for those already well established in theology *and* who showed promise in understanding Aristotle's challenging philosophy. It's as if Maimonides foreknew the synthesis of Athens and Jerusalem would be difficult for many to receive.

In *The Guide*, Maimonides puts forth the main problem of reconciling faith with reason: the over-anthropomorphism of God within the interpretations of Scripture. He offers an argument similar to that of his predecessor Philo. In the Torah, God is often referred to in human terms, but this should not lead us to believe that He has a body of any kind or that He acts in any way as humans do.

When Scripture says, "God will act with the power of his hand," Maimonides interprets this as a metaphor comparing a human king and God. God reveals Himself in this way for our benefit—to help us understand something of what an unknowable God is like by using familiar ideas. For Maimonides, God does not have hands and He does not write decrees on paper or ride horses to lead his army into battle. Though in some way, His action is something *like* this. The metaphors are there for humanity's understanding, a form of communication from an infinite being to mortal ones.

To strengthen his argument, Maimonides thoroughly analyzed the Hebrew action verbs used to describe God's works. He saw they were often homonyms, or single words used in two different senses. Maimonides believed one sense was used when referring to human actors and a second sense used when referring to God as the actor. The main point Maimonides makes here is that the stories of Scripture do indeed teach us something important about the actions of God; however, we cannot limit Him with human actions bound within time as we are. They are similar but different.

Moses Maimonides's contribution to the fuller understanding of the Jewish faith was massive. It can also be said that he played a large part in continuing the great conversation of Plato and Aristotle within the context of Judaism. Like Philo of Alexandria, Maimonides was strongly influenced by the rational understandings and terminologies of the Greeks. This influence spread far past Philo and Maimonides to eventually become intertwined within the larger context of the Jewish faith.

ISLAM

Islam is the world's second-largest religion, comprising 25 percent of the world's population with just under two billion followers. The title Islam translates as "submission to God," highlighting the focus of the faith, the worship of and submission to the one and only God—Allah. The Islamic tenets of faith are commonly referred to as the *five pillars*.

The Five Pillars of Islam

1. Shahada: The declaration of faith composed of two parts. There is no god but Allah and Muhammad is the messenger of God.

2. Salah: Daily call to prayer. Muslims pray five times a day by chanting aloud within the mosque and prostrating toward the holy city of Mecca. Verses from the Qur'an are read aloud.

3. Zakat: Almsgiving. Giving to those in need helps purify oneself through works of charity.

4. Sawm: Fasting. Fasting takes place especially during the month of Ramadan. Muslims refrain from food, drink, sexual activity, and smoking from sunrise to sunset.

5. Hajj: Pilgrimage to Mecca. Faithful Muslims are required to make one journey to the city of Mecca during their lifetime if they are physically capable of doing so.

Islam is a centuries-old faith that shares roots with both Judaism and Christianity. All three religions are monotheistic and all three claim Abraham as their universal father in faith. Where Islam stands apart is in the primacy it places on the Prophet Muhammad. For Islam, biblical figures such as Adam, Abraham, Moses, and Jesus were minor prophets who prepared the way for the coming of the fullness of truth given to the Prophet Muhammad. Unlike the Christian Jesus, Muhammad was not divine, but he was given the highest honor as the greatest and last of all the prophets. For Muslims, his message written down in the Qur'an is the clearest revelation of the truth, correcting all errors that came before.

Since the time of Muhammad in 570–632 AD, Islam, like Judaism and Christianity, has had its share of synthesizers attempt to marry the wisdom of Plato and Aristotle with the revelation of Allah. In fact, much of this synthesis occurred during a period known as the Islamic Golden Age, spanning from the eighth century to the fourteenth century AD, during which time Islamic thought reached one of its high points. Two Golden Age philosophers worked to combine faith and reason in a powerful way, and, in doing so, helped to permanently influence the interpretation of Islam. These two synthesizers were Ibn Sina and Ibn Rush'd, known as Avicenna and Averroes in the West.

Ibn Sina—Avicenna (980–1037 AD)

Avicenna was born in Persia in 980 AD and grew up in what is now Uzbekistan. From an early age, he showed prowess in studies and by the age of ten had learned the entirety of Islam's holy book, the Qur'an, as well as other important texts. As a teenager, Avicenna was introduced to the *Metaphysics* of Aristotle, though he had great difficulty understanding it at first. It wasn't until he stumbled across a commentary on the *Metaphysics*, written by an older Islamic philosopher, al-Farabi, that Avicenna's understanding of Aristotelianism blossomed.

Interestingly, the Aristotelian sources available to early Islamic philosophers like al-Farabi and Avicenna were most likely not purely of Aristotle. Many of them were combinations of Platonic ideas with Aristotelian ones passed on by the Neoplatonists of that era. Thinkers like Plotinus often combined ideas from the two great teachers in an attempted synergy. Because of this source-material issue, Avicenna likely ended up learning more of Plato's philosophy than he realized, though he believed it was pure Aristotelianism.

Avicenna spent long periods in study and prayer, attempting to reconcile the truths of Islam with the wonders of Greek philosophy in true synthesizer fashion. He saw both sources of truth as given to him by Allah, one from direct revelation and the other through natural reason. Avicenna grew up to become a physician, philosopher, and writer of immense influence within Islam. To highlight the importance of his ideas, professor of Islamic history Sajjad H. Rizvi has called him "arguably the most influential philosopher of the pre-modern era."[6] Avicenna's thought spread to a variety of fields and he is often credited as the founder of early-modern medicine, thanks to his extensive studies on the subject.

One of Avicenna's philosophical goals was to logically deduce proof of God's existence. In *The Proof of the Truthful*, he argues there must be a necessary existent for anything else to have existence: an argument he derived from Plato's Form of the Good and Aristotle's Unmoved Mover. In a nutshell, Avicenna's argument is this: Because everything that exists is reliant on something else to cause its existence, then there must be something that was first, whose existence is necessary and who begins the long chain of things coming into being from other things.

Following in the line of Aristotle, if everything comes from something else, you can't go back infinitely or nothing would ever have started existence in the first place. It's the infinite regression problem presented once more. Something had to have eternal self-existence for the long chain of caused things to begin at all. This necessary existence standing outside the chain of cause is what we call God.

Avicenna wove his faith into his description of this necessary existence by assigning it Islamic attributes. The necessary being must be a perfect unity just as Allah is one; it must also be immaterial as Allah is pure spirit and nonphysical in nature. The necessary existence must be all-knowing and all-powerful, just as Allah is said to know all things and have the power to move all things. Lastly, the necessary existence must be good in nature, just as Allah is only goodness and possesses no evil within Him.

The arguments laid out by Avicenna, and there were many, influenced theology and philosophy both within the world of Islam and outside of it. Moses Maimonides and, later, Thomas

Aquinas, for example, would pick up Avicenna's arguments and absorb them into their own respective belief systems to help in logically explaining the existence of Yahweh and the Trinity.

Ibn Rush'd—Averroes (1126–1198 AD)

The second synthesizer of the Islamic Golden Age was Ibn Rush'd, or Averroes. He was born in 1126 AD in Córdoba, Spain, just twelve years before the Jewish philosopher Moses Maimonides would be born in the same city. The thinking of Averroes, like Avicenna before him, had immense impact on the larger world of philosophy, though more so outside of Islam than within it. He was given the names the Commentator and the Father of Rationalism by scholars in the West because of his extensive commentaries on Aristotle. Professor Richard C. Taylor emphasizes this love for Aristotle, quoting Averroes as saying, "'I believe that this man was a model in nature and the exemplar which nature found for showing final human perfection.'"[7]

Averroes was so drawn in by Aristotelianism that he wrote multiple commentaries of every surviving work of Aristotle he could find—no small feat. He wrote commentary on Plato's *Republic* as well. His commentaries comprised short and medium versions, meant for the public, while the long commentaries were filled with pages of original thought and high technical detail aimed toward scholars of philosophy and theology. A similar approach to Maimonides's *Guide for the Perplexed*.

By the time of his death, Averroes had written over one hundred books on nearly every possible subject. These works included writings on medicine, astronomy, physics, psychology, mathematics, theology, law, and linguistics. He was a true polymath and genius of his day. Apart from the time he spent in intellectual pursuits, Averroes served as a prominent judge of Islamic law and as court physician for the Almohad caliphate in Córdoba.

Averroes was well versed in the thought of his predecessor, Avicenna; however, he disagreed with the amount of Platonism that found its way into Avicenna's thinking. As Aristotle openly critiqued the thought of Plato, so Averroes openly critiqued the thought of Avicenna. By the time Averroes came to study Greek philosophy, Islam had gained access to the original, pure works of Aristotle. When he saw just how much Neoplatonism had unknowingly crept into Avicenna's philosophy, Averroes determined to purify Islamic philosophy toward true Aristotelianism and spent the remainder of his life with this goal in mind. Interestingly, it is precisely the Islamic love of philosophy and preservation of Aristotle's works that led, in large part, to the European Renaissance through trade and intellectual collaboration. Europe's recovery of these lost texts spurred a period of great learning and synthesis as we'll see later with Aquinas.

In his attempt to combine philosophy with the faith of Islam, Averroes argued strongly that scriptural texts should be interpreted allegorically wherever they contradicted the conclusions of natural reason. Using arguments similar to those of Philo, Averroes writes, "We affirm definitely that whenever the conclusion of a demonstration is in conflict with the apparent meaning of Scripture (or Religious Law), that apparent meaning admits of allegorical interpretation according to the rules for such interpretation in Arabic. This proposition is questioned by no Muslim and doubted by no believer."[8]

With such an approach in pursuit of truth, Averroes did not

shy away from reading thinkers outside of the Muslim community. This practice did not come without heavy criticism from fellow believers, but Averroes pressed on nonetheless. He writes, "If before us someone has inquired into wisdom, it behooves us to seek help from what he has said. It is irrelevant whether he belongs to our community or to another."[9]

Though he valued reading outside his tradition, he began his search within it. In seeking to prove the existence of Allah, as Avicenna had attempted before him, Averroes read through all the doctrines pertaining to Allah from within the four sects of Islam and concluded that there were only two arguments from reason he could accept that also adhered strictly to the teachings of the Qur'an.

Averroes's first argument for the existence of God was that of providence. It says simply that the world seems suited for the welfare of human life, therefore there must be a Creator who designed it to be this way. His second argument was the argument from invention. This proposes that natural objects, such as plants and animals, seem to have been invented for their specific places in nature and perfectly suited for the environments in which they live. Therefore, there must be a Divine Inventor behind the scenes who made it so. Averroes believed that the only explanation for the beautiful complexity of life all around us is that there is an intelligent designer who intentionally made creation to be that way.

This argument continued to develop through the centuries and was taken up again by the naturalist philosopher William Paley in 1802 in his work titled *Natural Theology*. Paley continued in Averroes's line of thought with the introduction of his Divine Watchmaker. Paley writes the following:

In crossing a heath, suppose I pitched my foot against a stone and were asked how the stone came to be there; I might possibly answer that, for anything I knew to the contrary, it had lain there forever. Nor would it perhaps be very easy to show the absurdity of this answer. But suppose I had found a watch upon the ground, and it should be inquired how the watch happened to be in that place; I should hardly think of the answer I had before given, that, for anything I knew, the watch might have always been there. Yet why should not this answer serve for the watch as well as for the stone? Why is it not as admissible in the second case as in the first? For this reason, and for no other, namely, that when we come to inspect the watch, we perceive—what we could not discover in the stone—that its several parts are framed and put together for a purpose, e.g., that they are so formed and adjusted as to produce motion, and that motion so regulated as to point out the hour of the day; and that if the different parts had been differently shaped from what they are, or placed after any other manner or in any other order than that in which they are placed, either no motion at all would have been carried on in the machine, or none which would have answered the use that is now served by it.[10]

Averroes's reasoning is known as the argument of intelligent design today. Intelligent design believes the universe is too sophisticated, ordered, and complex not to have a designing mind behind it. Because science has discovered a multitude of new things about the universe since the age of Averroes and Paley, many believe this ancient argument now carries more weight than ever. An excellent, detailed summary of the modern argument for intelligent design is laid out in the book *Return of the God Hypothesis*, by Stephen C. Meyer.

CHRISTIANITY

The Greek philosophical conversation of Athens echoed in the halls of Christendom more than it did in any other religion. The force of influence came from the Greek philosophers, as well as from the Jewish and Islamic theologians who had taken up Greek ideas into their theologies. Interestingly, many of the patristics (church fathers from the first to fifth centuries) were educated in Greek systems and were learned in Greek philosophy, so much so that several were experts in the popular study of rhetoric. It is to one of those experts we now turn.

Augustine of Hippo (354–430 AD)

Augustine of Hippo is one of the best-known early thinkers to assimilate the wisdom of Athens into the Christian world. He was born in the year 354 AD, in what is now Algeria, and was of North African (Roman) descent. Augustine was a rational man, an intellectual raised with a Christian mother and a pagan father. He discovered a love for philosophy at an early age after reading Cicero's *Hortensius*—a work that has since been lost.

Augustine spent most of his working career as a professor of rhetoric until he converted to the Christian faith at the age of thirty-one. He attributed his conversion to the unceasing prayers of his devout mother, Monica. After his conversion, Augustine quickly became one of Christianity's most influential leaders as the Bishop of Hippo (a town on the coast of northern Africa). The Catholic Church recognized the importance of Augustine's ideas, honoring him with the prestigious title of "Doctor of the Church," an extremely rare endorsement.

Augustine is known for his preference toward Plato in the great conversation. He developed a specifically Platonic-Christian system of his own, though during his lifetime he may have had access to just one of Plato's original works. The bulk of his Platonism came from local Neoplatonists, such as Plotinus, whom he knew personally.

Augustine held Plato as the one philosopher who caught the clearest glimpse of the truth apart from the revelation of faith. In his work titled *The City of God*, Augustine wrote of his respect for Plato in particular:

> Among the disciples of Socrates, Plato was the one who shone with a glory which far excelled that of the others, and who not unjustly eclipsed them all . . . . For those who are praised as having most closely followed Plato, who is justly preferred to all the other philosophers of the Gentiles, and who are said to have manifested the greatest acuteness in understanding him, do perhaps entertain such an idea of God as to admit that in Him are to be found the cause of existence, the ultimate reason for the understanding, and the end in reference to which the whole of life is to be regulated.[11]

Later in life, Augustine would denounce his early love of Plato, though he continued to draw on Platonic and Neoplatonic ideas regularly. Augustine agreed with Plato and Philo that there exists a separate and more perfect world from the one we perceive with our five senses. For Plato, this was the world of the forms, worthy of our contemplation and highest regard. For Augustine, this was the world of Heaven and the things of God. *The City of God* presents human history as a conflict between the earthly city of man and the ideal city of God. In Platonic fashion, the world of the senses is but a poor and tarnished version of the world of heavenly perfection to which we ought to strive. The citizens of Augustine's heavenly city forgo earthly pleasures in pursuit of contemplating the Good, which for Augustine is God Himself, the source of unending joy.

Augustine garnered some ideas from Aristotle as well, though he likely had secondhand knowledge of them. Aristotle identified the highest power of humanity as its rational soul. It is our ability to reason and to *know* that sets humanity apart from the rest of the created world. Augustine continued this line of thought, claiming that the human soul is immortal, or that once created it never dies. It is a gift given to us by God. The rational soul provides us with the ability to see the things of Heaven and to know the things of God—a power given to no other animal.

Another of Augustine's important contributions to the great conversation were his thoughts on time and eternity. Eternity is an extremely difficult concept to discuss in any rational capacity, but Augustine offered unique ways of considering it. In Book XI of his *Confessions*, he presents the idea that while our minds remember the past and anticipate the future, in reality, neither one exists. Only the present moment exists, though for us the present passes by moment to moment. Augustine says that for God, time does not pass by moment to moment; rather, for Him, it is always the eternal *now*. The difference for God, however, is that He does not see one moment at a time like we do. Instead, he sees the whole of time all at once. For God, all moments—whether past, present, or future for us—are equally now. Augustine writes, "a long time is long only because constituted of many successive movements which cannot be simultaneously extended. In the eternal, nothing is transient, but the whole is present."[12]

Augustine was also one of the early minds to propose the idea that time and space did not exist before the act of creation. Building off the arguments of philosophers like Plotinus, he argued there was no empty universe just sitting around waiting for creation to happen. It wouldn't be until over fifteen hundred years later that scientists would come to prove what Augustine had already said.

Of the absence of any space prior to creation, Augustine writes, "The way, God, in which you made heaven and earth was not that you made them either in heaven or on earth . . . . Nor did you make the universe within the framework of the universe. There was nowhere for it to be made before it was brought into existence."[13] His ideas were compelling in his own time and have been handed down through the generations for good reason. When viewed in light of modern scientific discovery, however, they become prescient.

Thomas Aquinas (1225–1274 AD)

The second Christian synthesizer for our discussion is Thomas Aquinas. Aquinas had the unique opportunity of having access to the work of every philosopher and synthesizer who came before him, as well as pure recovered works of Aristotle. During his life, he compiled one of the largest comprehensive bodies of knowledge in his two major works, the *Summa Theologia* and the *Summa*

Contra Gentiles. He is commonly referred to within Christianity as "the Synthesizer" because his works brought together the thoughts of nearly every philosopher and theologian that preceded him, including Plato, Aristotle, Philo, Maimonides, Avicenna, Averroes, and Augustine. So influential were his teachings on the faith that the Catholic Church bestowed on Aquinas the honor of "Doctor of the Church," as it had with Augustine before him. He was then given the added title of the "Angelic Doctor" to acknowledge his teachings were enlightened by heaven. Aquinas is widely regarded in Western philosophy as one of the greatest minds who ever lived.

Thomas Aquinas was born in 1225 AD near the town of Aquino in Italy. He was born to a lower-prominent family and went to excellent schools early in life. When a military conflict arose in 1239 AD, he was sent off to the public university in Naples, and it was there that he first encountered the writings of Aristotle and the pagan philosophers. Greek philosophy changed the way he saw the world from that point forward. Aquinas argued vehemently against purists of Christianity in defense of the pagan philosophers' ideas. He believed, like the other synthesizers, that truth could be found in many forms, both secular and revealed. In fact, Augustine and Aquinas were prominent figures in a long history of Christians who believed that truth, wherever it is found, does not contradict Truth Himself (God).

At the age of nineteen and against his family's wishes, Aquinas joined a newly formed religious order known as the Dominicans. There he vowed to live a life of poverty, chastity, and obedience. As a Dominican friar, Aquinas held various teaching positions in Paris, Naples, Orvieto, and Rome. He was respected by many for his genius, though he constantly battled against others who disagreed with his ideas. His writings have lived on long after his death and are now held as the standard for Christian philosophy and theology. Aquinas possessed the rare combination of a superior intellect, a devout heart, and a wide accessibility to writings from all over the world.

While he read many different thinkers, there was only one philosopher who stood out head and shoulders above the rest: Aristotle. This love is evident in his writings as he refers to Aristotle simply as "the Philosopher," instead of by his name. Aquinas read every available page of Aristotle, which is no small task, and claims to have been given the divine gift of understanding them all on the first pass. There is even a legend that tells of a discussion between Thomas Aquinas and one of his Dominican brothers as they were standing together on a hillside overlooking a large city.

The brother asked, "What if you could own the whole of what we see below?"

Aquinas quickly replied, "I would rather be given the chance to read the lost pages of Aristotle."

Aristotle's influence on Aquinas and his philosophy is so deep that the two can no longer be separated out. Aquinas successfully integrated Aristotle, and many others, forever into what is now called Thomism and subsequently into the entirety of the Christian worldview.

Aquinas is famous for his attempt to prove the existence of God using logic, just as his predecessors had done before him. He settled on five basic arguments, known as the *five ways*, almost all of them stemming from Aristotle. His first three ways focus on the need for a First Cause or Necessary Being to explain everything we observe in the world—change, movement, causality, etc. His fourth way is that of gradation. Here he borrows from Plato saying, if we describe things as "better" or "worse," then those statements only make sense in light of a "best," and that best is God. His fifth way uses Aristotle's ideas of telos and Final Cause. This way suggests that things seem intelligently designed for a purpose or an end, and therefore there must be a Designer as well as a Final End toward which everything is moving. That Designer and Final End we call God. The five ways have stood the test of time and continue to hold weight today. They also help illustrate the tremendous influence of Greek philosophy on Christian thought.

Another of Aquinas's contributions to the great conversation is known as his *essence-existence* distinction. The concepts of essence and existence were put forth by Aristotle, and Aquinas carried them over into Christian theology. Hold on now, this gets a little heady . . .

Aristotle defined *essence* as that whereby something is what it is. In other words, something's essence tells us what it is.

Existence he defined as whether or not something actually exists. Something can have an essence, but that does not necessarily mean it actually exists.

To illustrate the idea, think of a horse and a unicorn. The horse has an essence and the unicorn has another essence. We know what a horse is and we know what a unicorn is, but this knowledge does not tell us which one really exists. Outside of our imaginations, the horse has real existence in the world while the unicorn does not.

From here, Aquinas took Aristotle's essence-existence discussion to a higher level. He derived that only within God, *essence = existence*. Consider that idea for a moment. In everything that is not God, there is an essence and a possible existence. For God, however, what He is (essence) is equal to what it means that

He exists (existence). He is being itself. Not an easy concept to grasp but fascinating nonetheless.

Aquinas interprets the story of the burning bush in Exodus, Chapter 3, with this Aristotelian idea. In the story, Moses encounters Yahweh (God) in a bush that, while on fire, is not consumed by the flames. Here God speaks to Moses, saying, "I AM WHO I AM." In this passage from the Jewish Torah, Aquinas recognizes one of the greatest philosophical statements ever made: God revealing He is existence itself. From this scriptural revelation, Aquinas would go on to teach that all created things find their existence as a sharing in the existence of God. The specific word he uses is *participation*. All things exist by participating in the primary existence of God—who is within all things, holding them in existence at every moment. Everything, from the tiniest atom to the furthest star, is held in being by sharing in God's first and necessary existence.

In the next chapter, we will turn our attention to Aquinas's description of the divine attributes—the culmination of Part I of this book. Thomas Aquinas was dubbed "the Synthesizer" for the good reason that he read, and synthesized, all the philosophers and theologians who came before him. Because of this, we now look to his description of God as our guide. In doing so, we also hope to find there a synthesis of many of ancient history's greatest minds.

CHAPTER 5

The Image of God

"It is easier to gaze into the sun, than into the face of the mystery of God."

—Hildegard of Bingen

Fable

As Sophia finishes speaking about the incorporation of Greek ideas into the theologies of Jerusalem, you look out over the city once more and take in the view. So much history here, so much depth of meaning consolidated into one compact piece of land.

"Shall we take a closer look?" Sophia asks.

"Yes, let's," you say, realizing that you're getting accustomed to new wonders on a regular basis now. You think to yourself, *How much more can this woman have to show me?*

The two of you walk down the hillside of the Mount of Olives, across a few streets, and into the Old City of Jerusalem, conversing and taking in the sights. Soon, you see the shining, silver dome from earlier rising high before you.

"Are we going in there?" you ask.

"Yes, this is the Church of the Holy Sepulchre, where all Christians, both Eastern and Western, venerate the site of Jesus's crucifixion, burial, and resurrection from the grave. Join me inside."

After you enter the church, your eyes adjust to the dim lighting and your nose detects the scent of centuries of burned incense hanging in the air.

Sophia guides you through the large expanse of the main church, explaining as she goes how Christ was crucified on the cross at one end of the church and buried in the tomb at the other end.

Fascinating, all in one place.

As you approach the site of the resurrection, you see a small chapel within the larger church marking the exact location where Christ emerged from the grave.

"This small chapel is known as the Aedicule. Within it are two smaller rooms, one housing the Angel's Stone, believed to be a fragment of the stone that sealed the entrance to the tomb. In the other room is the tomb of Jesus itself. This is the holiest site in all of Christendom and the place where Christians travel on pilgrimage from all over the world."

You spend time in the Aedicule chapel and then in the larger church, contemplating the gravity of events that took place here. Just before you leave, your attention is caught by a bright beam of light streaming down from a skylight high in the center of the dome above.

That must be the inside of the silver dome.

The interior of the dome has been fashioned to look like an image of the sun. There is a central, circular skylight allowing in real sunlight from the outside. Surrounding the skylight are architectural rays of light fashioned to look like large sunbeams. Looking at the image of the sun and its beam of light shining down on the holiest site in Christianity, you can't help but think of the connection to Plato's philosophy. The beam of light, the sun imagery, Plato's Form of the Good, God up above—it's all here, beautifully intertwined.

We have moved from the wonder of Plato and his Form of the Good to Aristotle's Unmoved Mover. From there, we've traveled through the main synthesizers of monotheism to learn how the thoughts of Greek philosophy melded with the theologies of Judaism, Islam, and Christianity. We have seen how rational thought has merged with the revelations of religion to paint a picture of God that can satisfy human reason to a certain degree.

We will now look deeper into the thought of Thomas Aquinas and his development of specific divine attributes. The image of God, as seen through the lens of human reason, arguably finds its clearest form in the thought of Aquinas. Though he was a cleric of the Catholic Church, Aquinas was known for his scrutinizing ability to find truth in pagan philosophy and religions other than his own. One of his greatest skills lay in knowing the difference between the revelations of faith and the knowledge of God arrived at by reason, and he went to great lengths to communicate the two separately.

The New Ladder of Nature

Recall from earlier the great Ladder of Nature described by Aristotle, each rung outlining an animating principle with successively greater powers of soul. Aristotle's ladder starts with inanimate objects possessing only matter and lifeless form, then moves up to plant life, beings with matter and a vegetative soul. These new vegetative powers include growth and reproduction. Third comes the animals with the added powers of sensation, simple consciousness, and movement. Fourth, we have humanity who possesses all the lower powers combined with our added abilities of reason, self-awareness, and moral decision-making. Last of all comes the divine spheres, on the highest rung of the ladder, where the heavenly bodies move nearest to the Unmoved Mover.

As an ardent follower of both Christianity and Aristotle, Thomas Aquinas built upon the Ladder of Nature to form his own version with only slight differences. The first four rungs are the same for Aquinas: inanimate matter, plant life, animal life, and the human rational soul. Above humans and before God, however, Aquinas inserts a fifth rung where he places the angels.

Aquinas admitted that the existence of angels is difficult to prove by purely rational means; however, he presents a solid argument for the added rung. Humans are bounded by matter and possess a rational mind capable of knowing higher things. God, on the other hand, is unbounded by matter, has no body, and is infinite in his rational knowledge. Angels, therefore, occupy the space between the two. Angels are unbounded by matter, meaning they have no physical body but are instead pure intellect and form. Their rational knowledge, while greater than humans, is not infinite like God's. They are in between on the ladder, unbounded by matter, yet bounded by a finite knowledge.

At the top of Aquinas's ladder is God Himself. God is the First Mover, the necessary being, and the one who shares His existence with all created things. For Aquinas, God's existence can be derived by reason alone. When it comes to describing what God is like, on the other hand, things get a bit more difficult.

He exists on the Ladder of Nature so far above our intellectual ability there are only a few things we can say about Him with any certainty. But this is where Aquinas shines. As philosopher Peter Kreeft says, he takes a limited foundation of knowledge and builds upon it a lofty tower.

TWO MODES OF KNOWING GOD'S ATTRIBUTES

Knowing God through natural reason is no easy task. Before we look deeper into the divine attributes of Aquinas's philosophy, it is important to discuss the two ways of knowing God that Aquinas believes are possible. For Aquinas, humanity cannot know concrete, positive things about God because He exists on an infinitely higher plane of being than we do. This means there is no way of saying things about God that carry any real meaning behind the statements. Revelation provides us with real knowledge of God, but the ascent of human reason cannot say much about Him of its own accord. While this is a discouraging limitation, Aquinas offers us two modes of knowing something about God: negative knowledge and analogical knowledge.

In negative (or apophatic) knowledge, we understand what something *is* by establishing what it *is not*. For example, pretend you grew up in Plato's cave and had never seen or heard of sunlight before. A person from the outside world could come in and describe it to you using negative terms to make it easier for you to grasp. They could say that the sunlight is the opposite of the darkness. Or, in the sunlight things are very easy to see, unlike your difficult-to-see cave objects. You don't know exactly what they mean by sunlight just yet, but your interest is piqued. It seems to offer something very different than the cave life you are used to. Negative knowledge says God is the opposite of evil and the opposite of injustice. You get the picture.

Aquinas's second form of knowing, analogical knowledge, allows us to understand an unknown concept by comparing it to similar concepts already known to us. To continue using our cave analogy, the outsider could compare the sunlight to your familiar firelight. They would describe the sunlight as being similar to firelight, though different in other ways. Sunlight is not fire, but it does share similarities with it. It can burn and it puts off heat, but in a different way than fire does. In analogical knowledge, we learn about an unknown by comparing it to something known. God is like a shepherd, like a vine, like light, and so on. Negative knowledge is *opposite* knowledge and analogical knowledge is *similar-but-different* knowledge. Within the framework of these two modes of knowing, Aquinas builds his image of God's attributes.

The Divine Attributes

There are five divine attributes from Aquinas we will use as our rational description of God. Aquinas provides more attributes than these five; however, I have selected these in particular because they encompass most of his main ideas and help to simplify our discussion. They are also the five attributes most recognizable in modern science, as we'll see in Part II. The five divine attributes are: God is *Nonphysical, One, Infinite, Eternal, and Unknowable*.

GOD IS NONPHYSICAL

I remember my systematic theology professor, Dr. Jeremy Wilkins, challenging us to imagine a nonphysical God. Go ahead and try it for yourself; attempt to picture God with your imagination. When my fellow students offered our thoughts, he shot each of us down one by one. Some students maintained a conventional view of God as an old man in a flowing robe riding on the clouds. One student conceived of God as an all-encompassing mist or ghost enveloping the whole universe. Another offered the image of pure light reflecting onto every part of the world.

"Unfortunately," said Dr. Wilkins, "you're all wrong. In fact, the very moment you try to conceptualize God with your mind you've already missed it. It is an impossible task."

My professor didn't raise this point to make the class feel foolish. Rather, he had the students go through this exercise to illustrate that it is an impossibility for the human mind to conceptualize a nonphysical God. No matter what preconceived ideas we may have of who or what God is, there is simply no way for the human mind to *picture* Him.

God is not physical; He has no body of any kind. The religious way to say this is to say God is pure spirit; however, this term means little to our rational sense. After all, what exactly is *spirit*? God is spirit, but more accurately, He is nonphysical and the opposite of physical things.

In the *Summa Theologia*, Aquinas explains the non-physicality of God in clear, Aristotelian terms. He writes:

> I answer that, It is absolutely true that God is not a body; and this can be shown in three ways.
>
> First, because no body is in motion unless it be put in motion, as is evident from induction. Now it has been already proved (I:2:3), that God is the First Mover, and is Himself unmoved. Therefore, it is clear that God is not a body.[1]

Notice that this argument is based on motion (i.e., change), as we saw in Aristotle. Aristotle's Unmoved Mover must put things in motion without itself being moved. Aquinas even used the same terms: "First Mover" (First Cause) and "unmoved." God, like the Unmoved Mover, cannot possess a physical body or he would be limited to time and change and therefore could not be the First Mover.

Aquinas then offers a second reason based on necessity.

> Secondly, because the first being must of necessity be in act, and in no way in potentiality . . . . Now it has been already proved that God is the First Being. It is therefore impossible that in God there should be any potentiality. But every body is in potentiality because the continuous, as such, is divisible to infinity; it is therefore impossible that God should be a body.

Here Aquinas relies on Aristotle's argument that all physical bodies are in potentiality. Bodies can be divided up endlessly whereas God cannot. He exists at all times, perfectly and fully actualized.

For his third argument, Aquinas refers to God as the highest (most noble) of all beings.

> Thirdly, because God is the most noble of beings. Now it is impossible for a body to be the most noble of beings; for a body must be either animate or inanimate; and an animate body is manifestly nobler than any inanimate body. But an animate body is not animate precisely as body; otherwise all bodies would be animate. Therefore, its

animation depends upon some other thing, as our body depends for its animation on the soul. Hence that by which a body becomes animated must be nobler than the body. Therefore, it is impossible that God should be a body.

It is impossible that matter should exist in God.[2]

GOD IS ONE

Our second divine attribute from Aquinas is the concept that God is One. Within religion, the idea stems from Deuteronomy 4:6: "Hear O Israel, the Lord our God is one God." That only one God exists is the main tenet of monotheism. Within the context of philosophy, however, the meaning is something more than that. While it may not appear at first to be a negative knowledge term, in reality it is. To say God is One is really to say that God is *indivisible*. He is unlike everything that can be divided up into parts.

In our experience, everything we encounter is divisible in some way. Let's look at ourselves, for example. Human beings can be broken up into distinct parts: bones, flesh, organs, blood, and so on. These can then be divided further into smaller chemical components and those can be divided even further into individual atoms. We can divide humanity in other ways as well, body and soul, for example. We are divisible, the world around us is divisible, but God is indivisible. He is the opposite of all division, being perfectly only one thing.

One of Aquinas's boldest claims was the statement that in God, *essence = existence*. Put another way, what God is, is the same as His act of existing. This is a major brain twister already—but hold on, it gets worse.

God is *one* to such a degree that what He is, is the same as what

He is doing (being is the same as action). What God is, is also the same as what God knows. To put it all together, God's essence, or what it means to be God, is the same thing as God's action, or what He is doing, which is the same thing as God's knowledge, or what He knows, which is also the same as existence itself. He is the definition of perfect unity.

Aquinas terms this perfect oneness and indivisibility of God as *divine simplicity*. God is the simplest of all beings and has no complexity whatsoever. There are no two parts, no differentiations, and no differences within God. If it were stated as a mathematical equation, it would read as follows: God's essence = What He is = What He is doing = What He knows = God's existence. While holding the highest place on the ladder of being, He remains, at the same time, the simplest of all things. Like Plato's Form of the Good, in God all things are literally one and the same. Perfect unity, perfect simplicity, perfectly one. This is why Moses Maimonides's second tenet of Judaism says God's unity is the like of which does not exist anywhere else.

Simplicity, for Aquinas, references God's composition, and is not an indication of His abilities or power. He writes of the divine simplicity in the *Summa Theologia*:

> The absolute simplicity of God may be shown in many ways.
>
> First, from the previous articles of this question. For there is neither composition of quantitative parts in God, since He is not a body; nor composition of matter and form; nor does His nature differ from His *"suppositum"* (concrete reality); nor His essence from His existence; neither is there in Him composition of genus and difference, nor of subject and accident. Therefore, it is clear that God is nowise composite, but is altogether simple.[3]

Here Aquinas lists for us the various distinctions that all created beings can be divided into. This is to show how God is not like this at all. We are divisible in many different ways, but He is indivisible. He is perfectly one thing. Aquinas goes on to give four more reasons why God cannot be made up of composite parts, but you get the main idea. Divine oneness means God is only one thing, indivisible, and the ultimate simplicity.

GOD IS INFINITE

The infinity of God is our third divine attribute, one that uses yet another form of negative knowledge. At the mention of the word *infinite*, our minds might move toward examples in the physical world—an extremely large distance, for instance, or an unbelievably large number of something. Still, whatever distance we conceive of or however many trillions upon trillions of things we group together, we regrettably remain far from infinity. So, what does this term mean when used to describe God? If, as we have said, God is not made up of any physical body, then it must mean something different when applied to Him.

For Aquinas, to be infinite means to be the opposite of all things finite. Perhaps it is better to say God is *unbounded* by anything, He is limitless and immeasurable, without beginning or end. This idea applies to what He is, as well as to what He does and to what He knows. Aquinas clarifies that God is infinite in His essence and not in any physical magnitude, ideas that are difficult for our minds to wrap themselves around. Again, in the *Summa Theologia*, Aquinas explains the following:

> All the ancient philosophers attribute infinitude to the first principle [God], as is said [in Aristotle's *Physics* iii]

> and with reason; for they considered that things flow infinitely from the first principle. But because some erred concerning the nature of the first principle, as a consequence, they erred also concerning its infinity; forasmuch as they asserted that matter was the first principle; consequently, they attributed to the first principle a material infinity to the effect that some infinite body was the first principle of things.[4]

In other words, Aquinas says many of the early philosophers thought that some type of matter was the first principle of all things and so mistakenly applied infinity to this matter. He clarifies that infinity is a different idea altogether when applied to a nonphysical God.

Aquinas continues after the previous quote moving into the idea of infinity proper.

> We must consider therefore that a thing is called infinite because it is not finite. Now, matter is in a way made finite by form, and the form by matter. Matter indeed is made finite by form, inasmuch as matter, before it receives its form, is in potentiality to many forms; but on receiving a form, it is terminated by that one. Again, form is made finite by matter, inasmuch as form, considered in itself, is common to many; but when received in matter, the form is determined to this one particular thing.... Now being is the most formal of all things, as appears from what is shown above. Since therefore the divine being is not a being received in anything, but He is His own subsistent being as was shown above (I:3:4), it is clear that God Himself is infinite and perfect.[5]

The previous quote is a bit tricky, but Aquinas uses the Aristotelian argument that all created things are made up of matter and form, having a material cause and a formal cause. Aquinas explains that matter is bounded and limited by the form it takes on. In the same way, forms are limited by the matter they inform. Matter and form both become bounded and limited by each other. God, however, is not like this. He does not receive any form and He is not made up of any physical matter.

As humans, we know finite (bounded, limited) things only. We have difficulty imagining what an infinite being is like because there is no example of infinitude to observe with our senses. When religion says, "God is everywhere," they are correct because He is unbounded by space. When they say, "God is all-knowing," they are correct because He is unlimited in what He knows. And when they say, "God is all-powerful," they are correct because His action is unrestrained in any way. God is infinite in everything—in His essence, in His knowledge, and in His power. He is completely unbounded, unlimited, and unrestrained in every way. Truly a wonder to consider.

GOD IS ETERNAL

Our fourth divine attribute from Aquinas is that of God's eternity. Here we find another term familiar to the modern ear. It also happens to be one more negative knowledge way of knowing what God is not. The word *eternal* stems from the Latin word *aeternus*, which means "without beginning or end." The world of faith uses this term to describe God as the being who has always existed and who will exist for all time, or, as Revelation 1:4 puts it, "him who is, and who was, and who is to come . . ."

God's eternity means He is unconstrained by time. Bundled in with this idea of God's separation from time comes the idea that He is also unchanging. As physical beings, we age linearly, continually growing older until we one day pass away and return to dust. Other physical things undergo change and corruption in similar ways. God, on the other hand, is the opposite of all of this. He does not live in a process of linear progression; He does not change in any way and He does not eventually pass away. We don't really know what it means to be eternal, but we can get an idea of what the opposite is like.

When attempting to conceptualize eternity, our brains can only imagine a really, really, *really* long time. However, it might be helpful to think of eternity as simply the present moment, the right now. This may be closer to how God experiences time—the next moment never comes; instead all moments of time are equally now. He exists in the past, the present, and all points in the future at one and the same time, in the eternal now.

A helpful image I've come across is to think of time as a large, tightly wound spring standing upright. Time moves along the spring from the bottom to the top, following along the coils one after the other, steadily ascending. Time has a beginning and it may also have an end. Now picture God as a light placed in the middle of the spring. The light standing in the middle has visibility to all points of time along the spring. We move along time in a linear manner, but God stands eternally present to all points of time simultaneously. An imperfect analogy but one that helped me gain some insight into time and eternity.

Aquinas's *Summa* says this of God's eternity:

> As we attain to the knowledge of simple things by way of compound things, so must we reach to the knowledge of eternity by means of time, which is nothing but the

numbering of movement by "before" and "after." For since succession occurs in every movement, and one part comes after another, the fact that we reckon before and after in movement, makes us apprehend time, which is nothing else but the measure of before and after in movement. Now in a thing bereft of movement, which is always the same, there is no before or after. As therefore the idea of time consists in the numbering of before and after in movement; so likewise in the apprehension of the uniformity of what is outside of movement, consists the idea of eternity.[6]

Aquinas follows in the footsteps of Augustine in his discussion of time and eternity. For God, there is no yesterday or tomorrow; there is only today. Time does not pass by as it does for us. There is only the eternal now. When people ask the question, "What was God doing before He created the world?" they are thinking in terms of a God bound by time. The reality is He was doing what He is doing right now and what He will always be doing—He is God being God eternally.

GOD IS UNKNOWABLE

The final attribute for our consideration is the idea that God is ultimately a mystery. As if we haven't discussed this enough already, it is an important reminder that while our minds attempt the journey toward knowing God, it is an endless quest. Judaism communicated this idea with their unpronounceable name for God. Known as the Tetragrammaton, the name was spelled with four consonants and no vowels, in English represented as YHWH, rendering it unpronounceable in speech. In place of the name of God, other words were used, like *Lord*. To say the real name of God was to make the false assumption that you could understand His mystery and know Him for what He is.

Aquinas makes it clear that in this life, "Reason cannot reach up . . . to know 'what it [God] is'; but it can know 'whether it [God] is.'"[7] We can know with reasonable certainty that God exists by means of the journey taken by the philosophers of old. But when we attempt to fully understand what God is, we hit the wall of unknowing. What it means to be God remains a mystery veiled from our sight.

The promise of religion, however, is that we will one day see God's essence face-to-face. It is specifically our natural desire to know truth and to know the cause of things that Heaven promises to fulfill. Of this promise, Aquinas writes this:

> Therefore some who considered this, held that no created intellect can see the essence of God. This opinion, however, is not tenable. For as the ultimate beatitude [happiness] of man consists in the use of his highest function, which is the operation of his intellect; if we suppose that the created intellect could never see God, it would either never attain to beatitude, or its beatitude would consist in something else beside God; which is opposed to faith. For the ultimate perfection of the rational creature is to be found in that which is the principle of its being; since a thing is perfect so far as it attains to its principle. Further the same opinion is also against reason. For there resides in every man a natural desire to know the cause of any effect which he sees; and thence arises wonder in men. But if the intellect of the rational creature could not

reach so far as to the first cause of things, the natural desire would remain void.

Hence it must be absolutely granted that the blessed see the essence of God.[8]

The mystery of God as the First Cause and the Unmoved Mover draws our intellect in wonder to discover Him more. There is always more to learn and more to uncover, an infinite treasure that beckons us. Many ancient thinkers spent their entire lives in contemplation of the greatest mysteries, seeking an ever-deepening understanding of realities like the Form of the Good, God, and wisdom.

There is something refreshing about an unsolvable mystery. A source available at every moment to which we can return and ponder in greater depth. A place with no end to new insight. The Christian theologian Frank Sheed put it this way: "A mystery in short is an invitation to the mind. For it means there is an inexhaustible well of Truth from which the mind may drink and drink again in the certainty that the well will never run dry, that there will always be water for the mind's thirst."[9] This unknowability is the fifth attribute of God—the ultimate mystery.

The Image of God

We now have five divine attributes from Aquinas making up an image of God from negative knowledge terms derived over centuries. To summarize, God is nonphysical, one, infinite, eternal, and unknowable. It is a simple blueprint at first glance, though highly technical upon further inspection. Faiths of all denominations claim these traits for God, and rightly so. What ancient philosophy offered to faith was a foundation of reason upon which to build, allowing the various revelations to be interpreted through a rational lens. Science and faith, it turns out, can coexist in a real way. There is a continuing conversation to be had between the two sides.

From here we move into Part II of the book, where we will use Aquinas's second mode of knowing God, that of analogical knowledge, to discover the universe in a whole new light. There we will discuss how the three greatest miracles of modern science stand as unique replicas of the God of reason. The Big Bang, the evolution of life, and the miracle of the human mind each carry within them a strikingly similar pattern—the pattern of God's own image. It is as if God used His image as the blueprint for all of creation.

PART II

God's Image in Science

CHAPTER 6

The Universe

"Look up at the stars and not down at your feet. Try to make sense of what you see, and wonder about what makes the universe exist."

—Stephen Hawking

Fable

It is early morning on an ordinary workday and you're enjoying breakfast at the kitchen table. As you sort through your upcoming to-do list, you hear a knock at the front door. *That's odd*, you think as you get up to see who's causing this interruption to your morning. To your surprise, Sophia's now familiar face greets you with a smile as you open the door. She says hello and asks if you will join her for a morning walk. It's been over a year since your last adventure with her, and your to-do list quickly fades from mind as the thrill of this intriguing woman returns.

"Of course," you reply, and you're out the door to see what lies ahead.

Sophia leads you along the sidewalks of your neighborhood and then out toward the edge of town. The two of you catch up on life, enjoying the cool breeze of the morning air as you go. Before long you've left the houses and streets behind and find yourself strolling through an open field. Sophia brings you to the top of a small hill where the distant countryside opens out before you in a sweeping view. There she stops.

The sky is now getting darker instead of lighter, as though night is returning. Within moments, the morning light from the nearly risen sun disappears and you are left in darkness and starlight.

"Look up," Sophia says. "I want to show you something no one has ever seen before." You gaze up into the now pitch-black, crystal-clear sky and see the brilliance of the moon and the Milky Way galaxy stretching out before you. Even the lights of the city have faded and the stars appear more brilliant than you've ever seen in your life.

"I'm going to take you on a journey back to the beginning."

"Wow, to the beginning of what, exactly?" Your curiosity is once again aroused.

"To the beginning . . . of everything." She continues, "Don't worry, it won't take long."

For a moment, nothing changes in the tapestry of brilliant, tiny dots scattered across the sky. Then, faintly, you notice the stars seem to be moving. You rub your eyes to make sure you're seeing clearly. The motion is imperceptible at first, but yes, the stars are definitely moving, and in ways they don't normally move.

The stars accelerate in their paths across the sky. As they move faster, a pattern begins to emerge—they are all converging in your direction. They move as if drawn to the earth by an invisible tractor beam. The entire night sky is now heading in your direction.

"Don't worry," Sophia says, "things will get intense, but you won't be harmed." And then, as if to reassure your doubts, she adds, "I promise."

All around now, the landscape no longer looks like home. It is intensely hot and volcanoes erupt in the distance, spewing gas high into the atmosphere. The ground flows with lava, appearing like a scene out of *Star Wars*.

Then, right before your eyes, the moon dissolves away. It becomes a trail of dust circling the earth, giving it momentary Saturn-like rings. The ground shakes violently under your feet and an entire planet emerges out of the earth to the south of you. It then blasts away as if shot out by a cannon and quickly leaves your view. *Unbelievable.*

After a moment, you look down and realize that you and Sophia are no longer standing on solid ground. The earth itself is disintegrating from underneath your feet, leaving you both suspended in space where the earth once was. *"Intense" was an understatement.*

Neighboring galaxies grow larger and larger as they move toward you. Out in space are fiery explosions where massive stars ignite in great bursts of light and then separate out to form two new stars—galactic collisions happening in reverse. There are magnificent displays all over the sky as galaxies pull apart and return to their original building blocks. It is a fireworks show unlike anything else.

The remaining stars are uncomfortably close now. Then, they too begin disintegrating into cosmic particles. You are in utter awe, still very much on edge, but grateful for the opportunity to witness this marvel of marvels.

A red glow intensifies around you in every direction now, as if space itself is catching fire. You can tell the temperature has risen well past livable conditions, though as Sophia promised, it is not uncomfortable. She calmly grabs your hand. "Get ready," she says.

"Here comes the best part."

"*The best part?*" You feel unable to imagine what could top anything you've just seen. The entire universe has become white hot in every direction. Every star and every planet, now dissolved into their constituent atoms, are crushed tighter and tighter together as the universe shrinks in size. All that once was matter reverts into blazing radiation energy. Then, in the blink of an eye, the universe compacts into an impossibly small space and is gone.

You and Sophia stand once again on the hilltop in the new light of morning, your heart racing and your mind melted. There are no words to say, so you remain silent for a long time, recollecting what you've just witnessed. After a while, panic sets in as a fresh realization enters your mind. You're about to be late for work.

Raisins in a Rising Loaf of Bread

I remember clearly the moment I realized what scientists meant when they said the universe started with a Big Bang. I'm slightly embarrassed to say it wasn't that long ago when I finally understood what they were trying to say. You see, for as long as I can remember, I've thought there's always been a black, empty void of space sitting there doing nothing. Then, all of a sudden and out of nowhere, all of the matter in the universe exploded out from one single point to fill up the empty space. That was the "Bang" in the Big Bang, right?

The revelation came while I was reading Fr. Georges Lemaître's work, which was the first to use Einstein's equations to theorize that the universe began from one single point. To explain his theory, he used the example of raisins in a rising loaf of bread. The raisins being galaxies and the bread around them the empty void of space. As a loaf of bread rises, every raisin within it moves out and away from every other raisin in the loaf.

That's when it hit me. The empty void of space wasn't sitting there waiting for an explosion of matter to fill it. In the beginning, there was no void of space at all. The black emptiness is what expanded out from a single, tiny point, like a bubble growing rapidly outward toward infinity. Space itself, the empty void, is what is expanding and pulling every galaxy within it farther and farther away from every other galaxy. Like raisins in a rising loaf of bread. Perhaps the Big Expansion is a more precise term than the Big Bang.

This soon led me to a second realization. Before the first moment, there was *nothing*. As in *nothing-nothing*. No black, empty space just sitting there. No time passing patiently waiting for something to happen. No "thing" at all. My mind hurt at this point. To be honest, the realization continues to fascinate me to this day.

Recent Astronomical Discoveries

For centuries upon centuries astronomers and philosophers the world over believed the universe was, for the most part, static. In other words, the stars out there in space have been sitting in their current places since basically forever. Yes, they moved through the night sky during the course of the year, but they always returned to their places like dutiful soldiers.

Einstein even built his theory of relativity upon this popular assumption. It wasn't until fairly recently that a brand-new image of the universe has come into view, one that reveals the universe in continuous dynamic, expanding motion. With the advent of technologies that help us accurately measure distances and movements on an astronomic scale, we are discovering more every day about the universe and how it came to be.

CANDLE UNITS OF MEASUREMENT

To understand how we got to the idea of an expanding universe, we need to look back to 1908 when astronomer Henrietta Swan Leavitt was assigned the study of Cepheid variable stars within the newly photographed Magellanic cloud star cluster. Cepheid variable stars are stars whose brightness pulses from dimmer to brighter in the sky. After studying 1,777 different Cepheid variable stars, Leavitt discovered their changes in brightness all followed a set cyclical period. The Cepheid stars pulse at regular intervals within a set range of luminosity. This discovery presented astronomers with an important new tool to use in their research of the universe—a standard brightness measurement, now referred to as a standard candle unit of measure.

When we look far out into space, we can find a Cepheid variable and compare its observed brightness with its known brightness. The difference between the two gives us a surprisingly accurate measurement of the star's distance from Earth. This revolutionary method of measurement was further developed by Edwin Hubble in 1923, who based his work off the discoveries of Henrietta Leavitt and others.

Edwin Hubble, for whom the famous Hubble space telescope is named, is best known for two things—measuring distant galaxies using the standard candle method and using the color shifts in light waves coming from distant galaxies to determine the direction in which they are moving in relation to us. It is this second discovery that's confirmed our recent understanding of the universe originating from one point in a Big Bang.

We are all familiar with the colors of the rainbow; for a quick refresher, remember the anacronym ROY G. BIV from grade school. Red, Orange, Yellow, Green, Blue, Indigo, and Violet. The reason for this order is simply that white light separates out into every color of the visible spectrum due to differences in wavelength. Each color represents a different wavelength of light. This is clearly seen in the light diffracting through a prism. White light diversifies out into an infinite array of colors, but the human eye sees distinctly the seven familiar colors of the rainbow.

The red color at one end of the rainbow is the longest wavelength that the human eye can detect. If you go further, you will get infrared light, then microwaves, and finally radio waves; however, our eye does not detect these wavelengths as colors. On the other end of the rainbow is violet light. Violet represents the shortest wavelength of visible light. Go shorter than this and you'll find ultraviolet light, then X-rays, and finally gamma rays. But again, we do not see these super-short wavelengths with the naked eye either.

So how are the colors of the rainbow helpful in discovering more about the movements of galaxies in outer space?

Interestingly, the color that a galaxy appears in our telescopes tells us whether it is moving toward us or away from us in a phenomenon known as the Doppler shift. You recognize the Doppler effect in sound waves when the blare of an ambulance changes pitch as it races past you. For sound, the Doppler shift presents as a change in pitch, but for light, the Doppler shift appears as a change in color.

As a galaxy travels farther and farther away from us over billions of years, the light shooting back toward Earth from that galaxy has been stretched out so far that the whole thing appears red in color. The more a galaxy is moving away from us, the redder it appears in color. This also means that if a galaxy is moving too fast and too far away from us, the light will stretch beyond the visible red color into infrared. Then we would only be able to detect its presence with special infrared detectors. If the light stretches farther than radio waves, however, it becomes undetectable to us altogether. The amazing reality is there is so much more universe out there that we will simply never be able to see or detect, ever. It has moved too far away from us, too quickly, for the light to ever make it back for our detection.

Edwin Hubble had access to the largest telescope on Earth at the time: the one-hundred-inch Hooker telescope. Armed with the knowledge of light waves and the Doppler shift phenomena, he fully expected to discover some red galaxies moving away from Earth, as well as some violet galaxies that were moving toward us. Surprisingly, when Hubble looked out into space as far as anyone had ever seen before, he found no violet galaxies at all, only red ones. Every single distant galaxy was redshifted. This discovery meant that everything we can see in the sky is moving away from us in every direction. Some of the light is moving toward us, but the galaxies themselves are all moving away. Hubble confirmed through experiment what Georges Lemaître was proving in theory, that we live in a dynamic expanding universe like raisins in a rising loaf of bread. The previous held notion of a static universe looked to be defeated.

THE THEORY OF THE BIG BANG

In 1927, while studying at the Massachusetts Institute of Technology in Cambridge, Fr. Georges Lemaître became intrigued by Einstein's theory of relativity. Basing his calculations on Einstein's equations, Lemaître formulated the now widely accepted theory of the Big Bang. He postulated if we rewind the clock back far enough on a universe expanding out in all directions, then at one time in the distant past, all matter must have been compacted together into one small, singular point. He named this point the "primeval atom." The question *where exactly was the location of this very special point?* arises from this theory. Well, the answer is that it was everywhere at once.

When Fr. Georges Lemaître first proposed his theory, it was mostly ignored. Static universe supporters came out and attacked it altogether. For many, the idea that the infinite expanse of the universe was at one time compacted into a tiny point was very difficult to accept. Competing hypotheses came out to explain Hubble's redshift findings while attempting to maintain the old, static universe belief.

After World War II, there were two hypotheses that emerged as lead contenders. The first was Fred Hoyle's updated version of a steady state universe, a universe that continually produces new matter to make it seem as though it were expanding. The second was Lemaître's primeval atom theory. Ironically, it was Fred Hoyle who coined the phrase "Big Bang" while poking fun at his rival's theory on a BBC radio broadcast program in 1949.[1] After that, the name stuck and the Big Bang theory of the universe eventually won out over every other theory as supportive evidence grew.

The strongest evidence for the Big Bang came in 1964 with the discovery of what's called the cosmic microwave background radiation, or CMB. Lemaître theorized that if the universe was at one time compacted in one tiny place, then we should find radiation from this intense original state in the space all around us. As he put it, "The vanished brilliance of the origin of the worlds."[2]

Proof of the CMB occurred much by accident while Arno Penzias and Robert Wilson were conducting satellite communication experiments. The Holmdel Horn Antenna was created by the National Aeronautics and Space Administration, whose goal was to use large, aluminized balloons to bounce radio signals off. This would allow for a new way to communicate across great distances. Penzias and Wilson took their first measurement using the antenna on May 20, 1964, and noticed an excess of radio noise they were unable to explain.[3] On top of that, the excess noise was coming from every direction all times of the day and night. To reduce this noise in their data, Penzias and Wilson attempted to eliminate every possible source of the problem. They silenced all radio interference and then removed the interference caused from heat by cooling the detector with liquid helium. Still the mysterious noise persisted.

Finally, they discovered some pigeons had made their nest deep inside the twenty-foot horn receiver of the antenna. Penzias and

Wilson relocated the unwelcome guests and cleaned up the residual droppings from the antenna horn, assuming this time they had surely discovered the source of the unknown hum. However, after all their efforts, the mysterious signal remained.

Penzias and Wilson did not immediately realize they had just discovered proof of the CMB. It wasn't until they called a friend from MIT, Bernard Burke, that they learned about an unpublished paper by Jim Peebles on the possibility of detecting radiation left over from the Big Bang. What they might have stumbled upon quickly dawned on them.

Amazingly, Peebles along with his colleague Robert Dicke were working nearby at Princeton University. Penzias and Wilson invited Peebles and Dicke to come over and check out the excess interference in the radio antenna in person. Once the four men were together, the enormity of what they were seeing set in. They had inadvertently discovered evidence of the radiation left over from the very early universe.

If you look up an image of the CMB, you will find a large oval map colored with splotches of reds, oranges, yellows, greens, and blues. The map is a complete view of the farthest detectable universe that we can see from Earth's perspective. It is a thermal map with the various colors representing slight variances in temperature present when the universe was very young. These slight variances are what later led to the clumping together of matter to form the planets, stars, and galaxies we see today. While it may not seem impressive at first, looking at the CMB map is literally looking back in time as far as we can possibly see, to around 380,000 years after the Big Bang. The very existence of the CMB, more than anything else, confirmed what Lemaître and Hubble had proposed through theory and observation. We did, in fact, begin from a very dense and very hot universe, one much, much smaller than it is today.

THE FIRST MOMENT

It is fascinating how much modern science can tell us about what happened in the first moments of our universe. How can we possibly know what occurred at the beginning of time some 13.8 billion years in the past? Well, we obviously don't know for sure, but modern technologies like particle accelerators give us surprisingly accurate predictions of what the conditions may have looked like. Using these technologies, scientists can theorize about the state of the early universe back to about a tenth of a trillionth of a second after the beginning of space and time.

The Large Hadron Collider (LHC) in Switzerland is the most famous of these particle accelerators. Created in 1998, the LHC is a huge, circular underground tunnel spanning seventeen miles in circumference. It operates using superconducting magnets, cooled to near absolute zero, and a radio frequency (RF) linear accelerator that launches protons and other ions to nearly the speed of light. The collider propels ions in opposite directions around the circular tunnel and then merges their paths once maximum speeds are achieved. Multiple high-tech sensors capture the resulting ion collisions and relay the data back for analysis. These particle collisions in the LHC are as close as we can get to re-creating the conditions present at the Big Bang.

There is growing evidence that shows that in the very first instant, all things were just one thing. All matter, all energy, and all forces governing physics were combined into a temperature and pressure so intense that these different things were one and the same homogeneous thing, basically an intense form of radiation. The idea that physical matter can be the same thing as energy is seen in Einstein's famous equation for the theory of relativity, $E=mc^2$. Energy equals mass multiplied by the speed of light squared. This simple and beautiful equation tells us that, given the right conditions (c^2), mass can be converted into energy ($E=m$).

While science has discovered quite a lot about the universe just after the Big Bang, we likely may never know what things were like in the very first instant, right before a tenth of a trillionth of a second. This special period, from time = 0 to time = 10 x -43, is known as the Planck era. This measure of time, called a Planck unit, was named after the founder of quantum theory, Max Planck. A Planck unit represents the smallest measurable amount of time possible based on the restrictions of Einstein's laws of relativity. Since time is ultimately relative, the Planck time unit has become a consistent standard for measuring it. The Planck era, however, remains one of the greatest mysteries in all of astrophysics.

One of the reasons we will likely never know what happened at time = 0 is that space and time did not yet exist. This makes it impossible to apply the known laws of physics here. Rewinding the clock to time = 0 gives us strange results as we near zero—such as the universe's density and temperature both approach infinity. When these types of extreme conditions occur in our calculations, they cause difficulties. We've coined the name *singularity* to help describe these difficulties, but the term doesn't offer any real explanation as to how we overcome them. Singularity means this problem is a singular one and the normal rules don't apply here. In other words, it occurs only under these specific extreme conditions. Think of it as a placeholder for a calculational problem we cannot yet conquer.

Fr. Georges Lemaître theorized about the singularity at the beginning of time. He writes, "If the world has begun with a single quantum, the notions of space and time would altogether fail to have any meaning at the beginning; they would only begin to have a sensible meaning when the original quantum had been divided into enough quanta. If this suggestion is correct, the beginning of the world happened a little before the beginning of space and time."[4]

We can rewind the clock and learn an amazing amount of information as we look near the singularity of the first moment, but we cannot "see" into the very first moment itself. The veil is closed, as it were, and we cannot enter in. We know that matter, energy, and the forces of physics seem to become a unity as we approach the first moment. Everything appears to have begun as a single primordial atom packed with infinite potential.

A BRIEF HISTORY OF THE UNIVERSE

A split second or, more precisely, one Planck unit of time after everything began, the universe was still extremely dense, extremely hot, and infinitesimally small. Under these intense conditions, the four forces of physics as we know them (gravity, the strong and weak nuclear forces, and electromagnetism) act in strange ways. Cosmologists have begun speculating on this state of the universe using the grand unified theory, or GUT. The GUT says in the time directly after the Planck era, the four forces of physics existed in a unified state.

Katie Mack gives an excellent description of the GUT state

in her book *The End of Everything (Astrophysically Speaking)*. She writes the following:

> It's been known for some time that, even under everyday circumstances, electricity and magnetism are aspects of the same phenomenon, which is why electromagnets are a thing and why dynamos can generate electricity. This kind of unification is like candy to physicists. Any time we can take two complex phenomena and say, "Actually, when you look at it *this* way, they're THE SAME THING," we basically explode with physics joy . . . . Based on theory and extrapolations from what we see in lab experiments, it's thought that at very high energies, electromagnetism, the weak force, and the strong force all come together to be something else entirely, such that there's no way to distinguish them—they're all part of the same kind of big particle-energy mix governed by a Grand Unified Theory.[5]

As the infinitely intense conditions began to ease ever so slightly, differentiation occurred in the cosmos for the first time, and the cosmological unity began to separate out into an ever-evolving diversity of different things. Between 10 x -45 and 10 x -35 seconds, a period of intense inflation occurred to expand the universe out at a profoundly increased rate. Remember we are talking about the void of space that's expanding. At this period space was not the clear, empty vacuum it is today. Rather, at this point all of space was completely on fire and white hot. All the matter that would come to make up the stars and planets was present, though it was evenly distributed throughout space in a sort of energy-fireball soup referred to as a quark-gluon plasma.

This duration of time is known as the inflationary period because the universe expanded exponentially faster than at any other time since.

The first thing to differentiate itself out from the original cosmological unity was gravity. We don't really know what this would have looked like, however, since gravity is more a result of the curvature of space-time than it is a physical force in the traditional sense. After gravity's departure, further differentiation occurred to the other forces of physics. First the electro-strong force divided in two, forming the electro-weak force and the strong nuclear force. Next, another division occurred within the electro-weak force to create the final four forces we see today in our physics: gravity (the attraction between masses), the strong nuclear force (holds the nuclei of atoms together), the weak nuclear force (responsible for radioactive decay), and the electromagnetic force (acts between charged particles, as in electricity and magnetism).

This final division of forces, known as the electro-weak symmetry break, had major consequences on the universe we see around us today. The symmetry break allowed for massless fundamental particles to take on mass for the first time. Peter Higgs was awarded the Nobel Prize in Physics in 2013 for his work explaining this interaction.[6] Before this break, particles existed only in the form of energy, but after it the particles transitioned from energy into mass. This was the point when matter came into existence for the first time.

In the early universe, entire cosmological "eras" flew by in the blink of an eye. At time = 1 second, the temperature cooled enough for larger particles to form. Quarks, leptons, neutrons, and photons came into existence during this period. The universe was still not transparent, however, because space was too tightly packed with matter for any photon waves to travel freely as light does now. Light was still trapped within the dense soup. During this time, the nuclei of atoms such as helium and hydrogen started to form as the strong nuclear force drew particles together into atomic nuclei in a process known as Big Bang nucleosynthesis.

The universe was now a ripe old age of two seconds. From here on out the duration of time between distinct eras in the universe's development grew much longer. From time = 2 seconds to about 47,000 years, we saw the beginning of a matter-dominated universe prevail over the previous universe of radiation energy. There was now enough room for the newly formed matter to move around and merge with other particles as the temperature of the cosmos cooled to around 9,000 degrees Fahrenheit or 5,000 degrees Celsius.

At about 380,000 years came the origin of the cosmic microwave background radiation, or CMB. At this stage the universe had cooled enough to cause a process known as photon decoupling. Newly formed atoms released photons out into space, and light as we know it was born. The universe became transparent as the photons scattered and traveled unhindered through space in all directions. This "first light" is what we see in the images of the CMB.

The successive period, from 380,000 years to around one billion years, is known as the dark ages of the universe. In these dark ages, stars and galaxies had yet to form into steady sources of light in the night sky. There was only the initial photon release from the CMB traveling out toward the ever-growing edges of the universe. At some point, the massive cloud of matter moving in space began to cluster together into spheres. These first celestial bodies may have been massive beyond comprehension due to the sheer amount of matter available when they formed.

As gravity drew elements together into larger and larger spheres, the temperatures and densities within rose until they ignited into stars. This was the dawn of starlight that ended the dark ages. Some of these early stars may have had very short lifespans compared to stars of today, igniting and exploding as supernova in only a few million years. The universe was now alive with brilliance as it continued to expand in size.

Mass accumulated into clusters thanks to the force of gravity. Stars then combined into galaxies spiraling around immense black holes at their centers. Planets collided regularly until stable orbits fought their way through the chaos. The basic structure of the universe would be set for the next 12.8 billion years. Order out of chaos, space expanding out ceaselessly.

At about five billion years after the Big Bang, the galaxy we call home began to take shape. Our Milky Way is an average-sized spiral galaxy in the grand scheme of things, which is still massive. To put it in perspective, light takes one hundred thousand years to cross from one edge of the galaxy to the other, and it takes 250 million years for our solar system to revolve around the black hole at the center of the galaxy just one time.

At around nine billion years, an explosion of stars occurred within the young Milky Way and a protostar was born. Clumps of matter began orbiting around this new protostar, colliding with other smaller planets until the large outer planets—Jupiter, Saturn, Uranus, and Neptune—were formed. The protostar eventually reached critical mass and density for its constituent hydrogen to fuse with its helium, leading to the full ignition of our sun. It has burned this way for 4.6 billion years, making it right around midlife today.

Around this same time a Mars-sized planet, commonly referred to as Theia, smashed into the newly formed Earth. The collision was so intense that it instantly vaporized all of Theia along with a huge chunk of Earth's crust and mantle in the process. So powerful was the collision, NASA says, "when the young Earth and this rogue body collided, the energy involved was 100 million times larger than the much later event believed to have wiped out the dinosaurs."[7]

Much of the debris from this collision was sucked back into Earth's orbit while the rest flew out into deep space. The massive cloud of leftover matter circled Earth until it found a stable orbit. As it circled, gravity drew the debris cloud together into a smaller sphere, forming the moon we know today. When NASA space missions took samples of the moon's surface, they found it to be made up of similar material as mother Earth.

Fast-forward to the present day. The section of the universe we observe all around us from our vantage point on Earth is supremely massive. It is around ninety-three billion light-years across in diameter, containing as many as two trillion galaxies. We call this the observable universe since it is the only part of the universe we can see and detect. It may be helpful to think of the observable universe as the sphere of space around Earth where light has been able to travel since the Big Bang. What's crazy to fathom is that the total universe outside of our observable sphere is likely much, *much* bigger. There are estimates as to the size of the total universe ranging from 3×10^{23} times the size of the observable universe all the way to near infinite in size. The only problem is there's no way for us to know for sure.

What's more mind-bending to consider is that the void of space has continued its expansion in all directions. It is commonly known that nothing travels faster than the speed of light. However, there is one thing capable of greater speeds and that's the void of space itself. Only expanding space can grow faster even than light can travel through it. Amazing.

At the Big Bang, space began its expansion outward from one tiny point. But there is no evidence to tell us that it has ever stopped its expansion. In fact, from what we can tell by our regular observation of the universe, the galaxies are accelerating away from one another at an ever-increasing rate. This means that after at least 13.8 billion years of faster-than-light-speed expansion, the universe is likely so ridiculously huge that the only proper description would be to say it's nearing an infinite size. And growing larger every second.

God's Image in the Universe

Merriam-Webster defines an analogy as follows:

- 1a: A comparison of two otherwise unlike things based on resemblance of a particular aspect.

- 1b: Resemblance in some particulars between things otherwise unlike: similarity.[8]

As previously discussed, Aquinas's second mode of knowing God is analogical knowledge of Him. This knowledge occurs when we compare something known (a thing we observe in the world) to something unknown (God). There are certain things the two will have in common and other things that will remain different.

Earlier, we used the analogical example of the cave firelight compared to the bright sunlight. They are both forms of light and both aid the eye to see. One is millions of times brighter, while the other is dim by comparison. One is the result of a fusion reaction inside of a nearby star while the other occurs via the combustion of wood or other flammable material. Between the two, there are some things similar and some things different. We gain usable knowledge of the sun through the analogy of firelight and, likewise, we gain real knowledge of God through analogies like that of the universe. In this case, God is the sunlight and the universe is the fire.

We can now ask the question, "How is our modern understanding of the universe an analogy of the image of God?" To put it in terms of the divine attributes, how does our modern understanding of the universe reveal God as nonphysical, one, infinite, eternal, and unknowable?

As with all analogies, there are some things similar and others dissimilar. At the outset, we can say the main difference in our analogy is that the universe is a physical reality while God is spirit and nonphysical. In this attribute, the two differ greatly. In addition, God does not change or pass through time while the universe does exactly that: changes and exists within the boundaries of time. We have a solid approximation of when the universe began, as well as a good theory of how it formed up to the present day. God, on the other hand, possesses all His attributes at once in the eternal now. Acknowledging these differences at the outset, let's now turn to what is similar between the universe of modern science and the God of ancient reason.

THE UNIVERSE WAS ONE

Over a thousand years ago, Maimonides proclaimed to the world that God is One, with no other unity in any way like His. It can be argued that one place we see such a unity so oddly like that of God's own is in the first moment of the Big Bang. In the very, very beginning, the universe was indivisible and undifferentiated in any way.

$$\text{Mass} = \text{Energy and } F_{gravity} = F_{strong} = F_{weak} = F_{electromagnetic}$$

All matter was energy and all forces were combined into one. It is as if in the very beginning, God imprinted His divine simplicity onto the physical universe. Mass = Energy and $F_g = F_s = F_w = F_{em}$ just as within God, His essence = What He is = What He is doing = What He knows = His existence. There was nothing to be separated out in the beginning of the universe, just as within God there is nothing to separate out or differentiate. He has no parts, is ultimately simple and perfectly one, just as the universe was at the beginning of time. In this way, the universe, as God's creation, bears the Creator's image.

A second place we find an image of God's oneness is in the homogeneity of the larger universe. No matter where we point our telescopes and detectors into deep space, the incoming data is relatively the same—no matter where we look, we find a similar density of star clusters and empty space. There is a sameness to space in every observable direction. So it is in God; He is the ultimate simplicity, the same in every aspect.

THE UNIVERSE DISPLAYS INFINITY

Soon after the first moment, rapid expansion caused the unity of the universe to begin its long process of differentiation into constituent parts. Matter cooled, racing away in all directions, eventually forming planets, stars, and galaxies. The void of space expanded outward, where it continues its expansion today, reaching insane size proportions impossible to fathom, let alone measure. While the second attribute of God's infinity is hinted at in the infinite temperature and density at the beginning of time, it is in the enormity of the universe of today that we see God's infinity more clearly revealing itself in the physical world.

If there was ever an example of infinity for human minds to observe, it would have to be in the size of the current universe and in the potential size of the universe to come. By all accounts, space has not slowed down in its expansion rate. The opposite seems to be true as the bounds of the universe continue accelerating away faster and faster in every direction. The void of space is expanding in a never-ending attempt to reach infinity.

Will it ever get there? Will it finally reach an infinite size? The answer must be no, as reaching infinity is an impossible achievement for anything in the physical world. But the comparison to God's infinity holds true if we see space as forever attempting to attain it. In this light, it seems as though the universe was designed to imitate its Creator, both at its indivisible beginning and again at its infinite end toward which it forever moves.

Thomas Aquinas said God is infinite in ways unlike a very large number or a very large distance. It is His essence that is infinite. But the universe displays infinity as best it can within the constraints of physics and time.

The vastness of space is now so large our brains couldn't comprehend it even if we had the power to see everything outside of our observable sphere. It is not infinite in the same way that God is, but it is as close as the physical world can get and getting closer every day. The point, again, is that God's image is mirrored in the universe as it moves to be more like its Creator and Final Cause.

So, remember the next time you look up into a star-filled sky or see an image from the James Webb telescope of billions of stars stretching across an endless expanse of space, God may be revealing to you something of what He's like.

THE UNIVERSE DISPLAYS ETERNITY

Recall that the attribute of God's eternity means His existence is outside of time and separate from it. If the physical universe, while trapped in time, attempted to replicate God's eternity, I'd expect to see a really, really, *really* long duration of time passing. Interestingly, whenever I find myself lost in the wonder of 13.8 billion years since the Big Bang, I say to myself, *Wow, that seems like an eternity.* A span of 13.8 billion years is an absurdly long time for us, relatively speaking. But is it an eternity? Not even close. Here again, however, we are speaking in analogies, which help us understand. Humanity is the only sentient being we know of in the universe capable of receiving these analogies and seeing them for what they are. They are here for us to discover and for us to decode, as if God is speaking to us through our very science.

Given our relatively short lifespans of around one hundred years, a 13.8-billion-year-old universe is an unfathomable amount of time. Once again, our brains are unable to process time on these scales. Think of the one hundred thousand years it takes for light to cross our Milky Way galaxy just one time or think of our sun burning for four and a half billion years with five billion years left to go. Now, try to think of the ninety-three billion years it takes for light to cross the observable universe just once at its current size—all of it is simply impossible to take in.

To extend the analogy further, there seems to be no end in

sight for the universe's existence, at least for the void of space, that is. With it forever expanding outward, the most likely scenario for the "end" of the universe will be by heat death. The heat death theory states that at some point, the expansion of the universe will grow to so great a distance that no galaxy will be in the visible universe of any other galaxy. Katie Mack describes this theory as follows:

> A universe whose expansion is accelerating is, paradoxically, one in which the influence exerted by the things in it is shrinking. Distant galaxies being dragged out of the Hubble radius (radius of the observable universe) by cosmic expansion will become lost to us. Galaxies whose distant past we can see now will slowly fade into darkness like ancient decaying photographs . . . . The stars already shining will burn out, exploding as supernovae or, more often, sloughing off outer layers to become slow-burning relics, gradually cooling for billions or trillions of years . . . . When the stars have all faded to darkness, the ultimate decay sets in.[9]

After every star exhausts its fuel and burns out, their lifeless cinders along with cold planets and black holes will be all that remains in the void of space. At this point, the lights will "go out" forever. After another unfathomable amount of time in the future, even the black holes will die out due to the slow leak of radiation discovered by the famous Stephen Hawking. Add in another eternity after this, and it is thought that the basic building blocks of matter themselves begin to decay. At around 10^{33} years, protons will decay and matter will cease to be. All will evaporate away until nothing is left except darkness and final radiation.

The time scale for this scenario to play out is trillions upon trillions upon trillions of years. It's a near eternity of time. Even then, the empty void of space will still be left sitting there in darkness and silence until the end of time. It is in these cosmic time scales that the universe reveals to us something of the eternal God who experiences no time but sees all times at once.

THE UNIVERSE IS UNKNOWABLE

How is the universe an unknowable mystery just as God is the ultimate mystery? I have heard cosmologists discuss and debate what came before the first moment of the Big Bang. Ideas like multiple universes or an impending Big Crunch, where gravity pulls all matter back together again, are thrown about. In the same vein, there are theories discussed about what could lie just on the other side of black holes, as if they might be portals to new dimensions or advanced alien civilizations. While these things can be interesting to think about, the reality is we don't know if there was anything before the Big Bang. More importantly, we most likely will never know. The science from these singularities will probably remain forever unreachable. There will always be some element of mystery to the universe, something more we still need to figure out, like dark matter, dark energy, and string theory, for example—and that's a good thing.

The key to seeing God's attribute of unknowability lies again in the very first moment of the universe, at time = 0. The primordial atom of the Big Bang contained pressures and temperatures so intense scientists say the known laws of physics literally break down. It is the ultimate singularity in science. Our knowledge gets us very close to the beginning, but the whole of the truth is veiled from our eyes. And so it is with God. We can know that He exists, we can know what He is *not* through negative knowledge, and we can know what he is *like* through analogical knowledge. We can know more about Him through the revelation of faith and what He has chosen to reveal through His prophets. But even after all of this, we are unable to fully comprehend Him. His true essence remains hidden from our minds just as the first moment of the universe remains hidden from our science.

CHAPTER 7

Life

"Those who contemplate the beauty of the earth find reserves of strength that will endure as long as life lasts."

—Rachel Carson

Fable

You are on a much-needed retreat to the coast. One morning, before anyone else is up, you sneak off by yourself for a long walk on the beach. In the early light of dawn, the waves lap calmly down the shore. It is a serene scene. You stroll the beach in silence, hearing only the occasional seagull, the sand giving way under your feet.

You're soaking in the moment when, far ahead, a figure emerges walking in your direction. As the person nears, her face comes into focus. Once again, it is Sophia. She is barefoot and smiling her usual smile. In one hand, she holds the bottom of her dress to allow the waves to splash her feet. Her eyes are shining brightly.

"Good morning," Sophia says. "Care to join me?"

"Of course," you reply. "So good to see you."

Anticipation sets in. You have learned now that these visits are never dull.

"Excellent, I want to show you something new," she says.

You are happy to be walking down the beach with your friend. However, as the two of you stroll on, a dense sea mist sets in around you, making visibility quite difficult. Sophia takes your hand, offering her steady guidance.

"This way," she says.

Then, as quickly as it came on, the mist dissipates and is gone.

You look around to find the scenery starkly different. At this point, you shouldn't be surprised by it anymore. You are still on a beach, but it is definitely not the same beach you were walking on moments ago. The sand is now mostly black and feels coarser under your feet. You look inland to see nothing except jagged, bare rocks. You can see some rocky hills far off in the distance; one of them is smoldering like a spent volcano. There are no plants, no trees—nothing except dirt and rocks. The landscape looks like images you've seen from the surface of Mars: bleak and barren. You also notice the air is different now, and something about it makes it difficult to catch your breath.

"Where are we?" you ask.

"We have come to another beginning of sorts. Welcome to Earth, three billion years in the past."

"Did you say billion with a B? Wow, there's not much here."

"That is true. Come with me into the water, but watch your step," Sophia says.

You follow her out into the ocean shallows. Jagged rocks scatter the seabed, so you step carefully.

"Look down here," she says.

You look in the water and see an interesting column of sediment sitting just below the surface. *Okay,* you think to yourself, *it just looks like sand; what's the big deal?*

"That formation you see there is called a stromatolite and it contains some of the first living cells on your planet. They are currently preparing the way for all of life to develop on Earth."

"Preparing? How so?" you ask, now interested.

"These cells, and the multitude like them, will harness the power of photosynthesis for billions of years, steadily converting carbon dioxide into oxygen. They are slowly but surely making the atmosphere breathable for you," she replies.

Fascinating, you think to yourself.

Sophia continues, "Every plant that will ever grow on the earth and every animal on the land and in the sea owe a debt of gratitude to the work of these simple cells. In time, these cells will venture out and blanket the earth in grasses, trees, and flowers of all shapes, sizes, and colors."

"Very cool."

"Cool indeed," Sophia says, smiling. "That is the power of life."

Our home planet exists in a class all its own. Out of all the planets we can observe in our corner of the universe, Earth is the only one we know of that houses life. From small, green bacteria to towering cypress trees, and from simple ground worms to complex humanity, Earth boasts an abundance of stunningly beautiful and diverse living things.

The sheer amount of life we see around us often leads me to ponder, *How did this all begin?* The answer to that question from within the scientific community is that natural processes of chemical evolution allowed nonliving matter to become a living thing. From the world of faith and theology, however, the answer is God. God created life on Earth, as described in the accounts of Scripture. Here lies the greatest of difficulties to overcome in the discussion between faith and science. It has also been the most difficult question in my own mind as I have slowly come to the realization that we don't yet have all the pieces of the puzzle with which to form a satisfactory answer. Life remains a mystery to be discovered. Let's begin by looking at the science.

The Origin of Life

Abiogenesis is the term in life sciences referring to the beginning of life as the result of natural, chemical processes. It is defined by *Merriam-Webster* as "the origin of life from nonliving matter."[1] The extended definition reads, "A theory in the evolution of early life on Earth: organic molecules and subsequent simple life-forms first originated from inorganic substances." The main theories surrounding abiogenesis reveal an evolution of chemical reactions and nonliving compounds that led to life in its simplest form—namely, single-celled bacteria.

The key prerequisite to abiogenesis lies in having the necessary components for living cells, along with the necessary energy sources, together in one place for an extended length of time. After this, the goal becomes the construction of a simple cell wall, a membrane capable of keeping wanted material inside and unwanted material out. In his book *A (Very) Short*

History of Life on Earth, evolutionary biologist Henry Gee writes as follows:

> Life evolved in the deepest depths of the ocean, where the edges of tectonic plates plunged into the crust and where boiling hot jets of water, rich in minerals and under extreme pressure, gushed out from cracks in the ocean floor.
>
> The earliest living things were no more than scummy membranes across microscopic gaps in rocks. They formed when the rising currents became turbulent and diverted into eddies and, losing energy, dumped their cargo of mineral rich debris into gaps and pores in the rock. These membranes were imperfect, sieve-like, and like sieves, allowed some substances to cross but not others. Even though they were porous, the environment inside the membranes became different from the raging maelstrom beyond: calmer, more ordered.[2]

Other biologists believe the miracle of life occurred closer to shore, in shallower waters along the coasts. In these waters, UV light and lightning strikes continually pounded the earth's oceanic soup of preorganic materials with the necessary energy for life to begin. For millions of years, compounds such as amino acids and nucleotides mixed together by the trillions all over the world. Add in enough UV light and lightning and you get life, like something out of *Frankenstein*.

This theory was independently proposed by two separate biologists in the 1920s—Aleksandr Oparin and J.B.S. Haldane. Now known as the Oparin-Haldane theory, it says organic life could have been formed from the presence of nonliving matter combined with an energy source, such as UV light from the sun found along the coastlines. Oparin and Haldane believed that the precursors to cells as we know them were formed by spontaneously aggregating lipid molecules. As these lipid molecules joined together over time, they eventually formed an enclosed space—the first cell wall.

There is much debate as to which came first, the complex cell that then allowed for metabolic processes and replication, or the metabolic chemical reactions that then later allowed for the ability of self-replication. In either case, it was the combination of proto-cell, nonliving material combining with an external energy source such as heat or UV light that led to the first signs of life on Earth.

If this theory is correct, the process was most likely extremely slow, stretching out over hundreds of millions of years. As the ocean's waters were heated by the sun, the evaporative process brought chemical compounds up into the clouds, where they encountered lightning energy. When the cloud moisture then condensed, the charged chemicals fell back down to Earth and mixed once again with the chemicals remaining in the ocean. This process created a progressively denser life soup with chemical compounds steadily growing in complexity. The process continued like this for millions of years until eventually the four main compounds needed for living cells were present: lipids, carbohydrates, amino acids, and nucleic acids.

In 1952, Stanley Miller and Harold Urey set out to re-create these conditions of the early Earth in an attempt to make living cells once again from nonliving matter. To do this, Miller and Urey crafted an ingenious two-beaker system that simulated the chemical makeup of the primitive atmosphere to the best of their knowledge at the time. The experiment worked by connecting the two beakers with tubing to form a closed-loop system. One beaker was filled halfway with water, methane, ammonia, and hydrogen to simulate the elements thought to have been present in the waters of the early Earth. The second beaker was slightly elevated above the water-filled one. This beaker contained two electrodes emitting a continuous spark between them, simulating lightning strikes. One beaker became the ocean, the other one the clouds.

For their experiment, the beaker containing water and chemicals was heated to activate the evaporation process. From there, the chemicals traveled up through the tubing and over to the second, elevated beaker with the electrodes. The vapor passed through the charged electrodes, where it received infusions of electricity. As the charged vapor cooled, it dripped down as "rain" into the tubing below and flowed back into the original water-filled beaker to complete the circuit.

This process was run continuously for one week with very interesting results. At the end of the week, the water in the beakers had turned a nearly opaque, deep red color. When the red water was analyzed, Miller and Urey found it contained five amino acids, including glycine, a-alanine, b-alanine, aspartic acid, and a-aminobutyric acid.[3] While they did not successfully re-create a living cell in their experiment, the two scientists did succeed in creating multiple compounds necessary for life.

In 2007, after the death of Stanley Miller, the original contents of the beakers were re-examined using updated technology. Scientists found there were more than twenty amino acids created in the experiment and not just five as initially thought. We now know that the early Earth's atmosphere was slightly different in composition than what Miller and Urey believed in 1952. Modern experiments like Miller and Urey's produce even more complex compounds than ever before. To date, however, we are still unable to re-create the miracle of a living cell in our labs.

LUCA: ONE MOTHER

Modern science holds that all living things are related to one another. Consider the immense diversity of life on Earth today—fungus, insects, trees, birds, dogs, humans. Would it surprise you to know that every living thing on the planet shares at least 20 percent of their DNA with every other living thing? Some share much more than that. Humans and apes, for example, share an astonishing 98 percent of their DNA. Because of this, evolutionary biology believes organic life likely started from one common origin point. Darwin foresaw this and wrote, "I should infer from analogy that probably all the organic beings which have ever lived on this Earth have descended from some single primordial form, into which life was first breathed."[4] Science has given a name to this *primordial form*, the seed of the tree of life, the great ancestor of all living things. It is called LUCA—the last universal common ancestor.

Life's universal common ancestor was most likely not the first bacterial cells that formed in the primordial oceans, though it came soon after, dating back some 3.5–3.8 billion years. In appearance, it would most likely resemble a modern bacterium. However, it would have been simpler in its intracellular workings and metabolic functions than the more complex bacteria we have on Earth today. Imagine, if you will, simple cells containing within them the potential to develop into every living thing you see around you today. Every fungi, fish, bird, plant, and animal. In a way, they were the ultimate stem cells.

The field of study tracing life back to LUCA is known as phylogenetics. This field blossomed in the twenty-first century thanks to advances in gene-tracing technologies. We have now cataloged the genetic codes from a myriad of plants, animals, and microbes into a vast library. This large collection of genetic data allows us to look deeper into the various genetic lines of biology to see where the codes are similar and where they differ. By following the patterns between genes, we can trace likely evolutionary paths all the way back to LUCA.

In 2016, Bill Martin and his colleagues, Madeline Weiss, Filipa Sousa, Natalia Mrnjavac, Sinje Neukirchen, Mayo Roettger, and Shijulal Nelson-Sathi, published a paper in *Nature Microbiology* summing up contemporary discoveries about LUCA, as well as an updated version of the branches of the tree of life. Through their research, Martin and his team uncovered a genetic phenomenon called lateral gene transfer, or LGT. This evolutionary event occurs when genes spread laterally between branches on the tree of life rather than through reproduction on the same branch. Lateral spread can happen through a variety of different mechanisms, such as viruses jumping from one life-form to another or through environmental stressors that cause cells to open and accept new DNA from outside sources. These phenomena introduce new, foreign genes into existing genetic codes.

Based on this knowledge of LGT, Martin's team sought to look anew at the longest lineages of biological life. What they found was a group of about 355 ancient genes, which they determined had not swapped branches laterally. "While we were going through the data, we had goosebumps," Martin recalls, "because it was all pointing in one very specific direction."[5] These 355 ancient genes were the observable remnants of LUCA.

BIOLOGIC EVOLUTION

Chemical evolution first brought about living cells from nonliving matter. Sometime after, LUCA developed out of these first single cells. From this point on, however, a new process took over as the guiding force of life. After life on Earth began, the long, slow progression of biologic evolution took hold of its development and never let go. Biologic evolution is the long and tediously slow process of miniscule changes to each generation within a species. The theory says that, given enough time—and we're talking a *long* time—one species eventually changes into another. This is the meaning behind Darwin's famous book title, *On the Origin of Species*, which introduces the concept that the origin of any species is the life-form right before it on the long line of evolutionary change.

Prominent scientists once believed a species came into existence fully developed and remained that way until it reached extinction. Each species of plant or animal was independent from the rest of life. This thinking is what led to the thousands of species-unique classifications and groupings we have in the fields of biology and botany today.

Darwin argued against this commonly held belief. He proposed that one species will morph into another due to the demands of its environment and resulting natural selection. He suggested that rather than being static and unchanging, every species was in a state of constant change, from the simplest of cells to the most complex mammals. For Darwin, the world of plants and animals we see today is like a snapshot, a single point in time on the larger continuum of continuous evolutionary change.

In evolutionary theory, there are two main mechanisms of action that cause one species to change into another. The first of these mechanisms is called genetic variation. Genetic variations arise when parents produce offspring with minor differences. The second cause is that of natural selection. Natural selection results from the stresses an environment places on a plant or animal population. Whichever sibling in a litter is best suited for that specific environment will win out in the game of life and subsequently reproduce more of its kind. Genetic variation occurs through reproduction, while natural selection arises from the external environment.

Genetic Variation

When two plants or animals produce offspring, the new generation comes out with minor differences from their parents. The siblings end up slightly different from one another as well. Some babies are larger, some smaller. Some have new eye colors; some retain their parents' pigment. One may have a robust immune system, while another's is weaker. Whenever parents mate, whether plant or animal, their DNA recombines to create one of a variety of possible concoctions. This is why biological siblings have clear differences, despite spawning from the same genetic sources. This event is known as genetic shuffling and accounts for the variation in a given generation.

The mixing of genes also occurs when plants or animals migrate into new areas. For example, if one group of bears wanders into the territory of another group, the locals might mate with the newcomers. When biologically diverse bear clans mate, a new range of genetic outcomes become possible. These new genetic mixtures may be insignificant in the short term, like slight alterations of size or fur color. But over centuries, miniscule changes add up to noticeable distinctions.

Take for example the pygmy mammoths of California. For millennia, massive mammoths roamed North America. About forty thousand years ago, some of these fourteen-feet-tall behemoths ended up on what are now known as the Channel Islands, off the coast of Southern California. With much less room to roam, the fittest mammoths were no longer the largest, but the smallest. Smaller mammoths could more easily survive on the islands' limited resources than their megalithic parents. Over the course of generations, the mammoths on the Channel Islands grew smaller and smaller in order to survive. Fossil records suggest the pygmy mammoths eventually averaged only two thousand pounds—which seems big until you consider their direct ancestors weighed in at twenty thousand pounds.[6]

Another way genetic variation occurs from parent to offspring is through gene mutations. Spontaneous genetic mutations happen while the DNA replicates within a cell's nucleus. Small errors in chromosomal separation or recombination can lead to changes within the new cell. This mutation produces some difference in the organism, which may pass on to further generations. These "random" gene mutations aren't always by chance, however. Sometimes, external environmental factors like toxins can increase the probability of mutations occurring.

Natural Selection

The second half of Darwin's evolution equation is natural selection. Natural selection refers to the weeding out of "unfit" animals by their environments. Take the previous example of giant mammoths stuck on a small island with limited resources. The smallest animals become the best fit for their new environment and the island ends up weeding out the larger siblings.

Take as another example: Fast cheetahs capable of catching gazelles thrive in the Sahara and weed out the slowest members of the gazelle population. Subsequently, the gazelles will necessarily adapt over time, becoming faster and faster to avoid the cheetahs. The cheetahs that can't keep up will then die off from lack of food. Natural selection weeds out the slow cheetahs and the slow gazelles, the weakest links among both predators and prey.

The most famous example of evolution from *On the Origin of Species* is Darwin's finches. While traveling to the isolated Galapagos Islands, Darwin noticed that the birds on each island had uniquely shaped beaks—distinct from those on the other islands and from those on the mainland. In total, he identified four separate Galapagos finch beaks. The birds were nearly identical in every other way to each other as well as to their mainland cousins. As it turns out, the birds on the isolated islands were undergoing something of an evolutionary experiment, undiscovered until Darwin's boat docked at the shores.

For reasons not completely known, the finches each remained on their own islands through many generations. Over hundreds, or possibly thousands, of years, each island environment shaped the finches in its own way. When Darwin arrived in 1835, he noticed that the variations in beak shape and size correlated with the differences in each island's food supply.

One island of finches developed large, thick beaks suitable for cracking nuts because nuts were the main food source on that island. On another island, the finches developed long, slender beaks perfect for grabbing insects hiding in the foliage. A third group developed the fascinating ability to hold sticks in their beaks with the aim of prying their prey from small holes in the trees. The finches that adapted beaks incompatible with an island's main food source died off, while the finches with island-specific advantages prospered.

Cooperation

Scientists have long known that genetic variation and natural selection are the two main forces driving the evolutionary process. However, there is exciting new research revealing a third cause also at work—that of cooperation. Harvard mathematician and biologist Dr. Martin Nowak has spent the last few decades studying mathematical models of the evolutionary process and has reached a startling discovery: Cooperation between organisms appears to be the most important factor in life succeeding and advancing.

Dr. Nowak notes that cooperation occurs at every step along the evolutionary process. It happened when nonliving matter came together to bring about the first living cells. It occurs between cells in the development of new organisms, and it's necessary in every animal population in order to advance the greater good of the group. There is a regular self-giving and self-sacrificing occurring within life at every level that leads to life's advancement.

In his book *Beyond*, Dr. Nowak writes of evolutionary cooperation, "A new view of evolution solves the problem: evolution is not only competition it is both competition and cooperation. From the dawn of time evolution included cooperation—the quest for cooperation is as old and fundamental as evolution itself. The call for cooperation is ubiquitous. Then we can talk of natural cooperation as well as natural selection."[7]

One fascinating example of life's cooperation can be seen in a forest of trees. Using an intricate system of communication, the trees of a forest can actually "look out" for one another and release specific chemicals into the air when attacked by hungry insects. The chemicals warn neighboring trees of the threat, signaling them to release bitter chemicals that render their leaves undesirable to the insects headed their way.

Trees can also offer aid to others who have fallen. Some have the ability to direct individual resources toward the stump of a tree in need and, in doing so, can effectively bring it back to life. It is a wonder to consider. Peter Wohlleben discusses these natural phenomena in his book *The Hidden Life of Trees*. He writes, "Why are trees such social beings? Why do they share food with their own species and sometimes even with competitors? The reasons are the same as for human communities: there are advantages to working together."[8]

Genetic variation presents life with countless new options for development. Those offspring well adapted to a given environment will survive, reproduce, and extend their lineage. Add in the power of biologic cooperation to these successful populations and life gains the ability to advance through individual sacrifice for the greater good. Multiply all of these factors by millions of different plant and animal species in millions of varied environments over billions of years and life becomes vastly diverse as we find it today.

BRANCHES IN THE TREE OF LIFE

According to evolutionary theory, the steady process of cumulative change took hold of LUCA and never let go, though life did not evolve in a straight line. Rather, it branched out from LUCA in many directions, forming what we call the tree of life. LUCA birthed descendants who changed, mutated, and adapted to their surroundings. Simple cells became more complex. Complex cells grew into multicellular groups. Some groups gained the ability to devour the elements around them while others harnessed the power of the sun through photosynthesis. Other LUCA cell lines accessed mineral content from the water to form hard shells of protection. While many of the branches died out and became extinct, three major branches survived to create the diversity of life we see today. These three main branches are bacteria, archaea, and eukarya.

Bacteria and archaea are both single-celled microorganisms made from prokaryotic cells. They share so many similarities they were once thought to be of the same branch on the tree of life. This all changed in 1977 when Carl Woese discovered the major differences that set archaea apart from bacteria. Woese found that the two groups have different cell wall compositions, as well as differences in ribosomal RNA sequences. These newly discovered differences were substantial enough to give archaea their very own branch on the tree.

It is the third branch, eukarya, where we find all the plants and animals we see every day. The eukarya branch is home to many unicellular organisms, as well as fungi, plants, animals, and even humanity. All eukaryotes are composed of eukaryotic cells containing a membrane-bound nucleus. While the prokaryotes—bacteria and archaea—immensely outnumber the eukaryotes on our planet, the eukaryotes stand out thanks to their larger size and visibility to the naked eye. The eukaryotes include all the familiar living organisms we think of when we say the terms *plants* and *animals*.

There are many smaller branches stemming off the main eukaryote branch. Red and green algae blooming throughout the oceans, fungi, and sea sponges are one of these. Eventually, this ocean life moved onto land and evolved into flowering plants and towering trees, blanketing the whole Earth in green. Corals and flat worms appeared as one of the first animal branches of eukaryote. These later evolved into a group of animals known as protostomes. This group went on to become crabs, spiders, beetles, butterflies, snails, and the slimy worms crawling through our gardens.

Fish grew out of a different branch in the eukaryote tree of life. During a period of evolutionary history known as the Cambrian explosion, some of the ocean's life-forms developed a spinal nerve system. Later, this nerve system grew into a spinal cord complete with a protective vertebral column. This new development led to the first-known fish, the jawless agnatha. Our modern-day lamprey would be the closest relative to these original fish. Out of these jawless fish arose all the bass, eels, salmon, and sharks swimming around our planet today.

Out of yet another branch in the tree of life, amphibians and reptiles formed. Salamanders, frogs, lizards, and snakes grew from early aquatic life-forms and later developed the ability to breathe air on land. At this point in Earth's history, the oceans were full of complex species while land life was limited to simpler plants and insects. The oceans were likely highly competitive environments for food, while the land was a veritable buffet waiting for sea-dwellers to evolve legs, lungs, and appetites for the feast.

The transition from fish swimming in the ocean to animals

walking on land was a long process. Biologists believe it looked something like this: Fish developed lobed fins and began to hunt around the shallow waters near the shore. Their swim bladder, or air-filled buoyancy organ, most likely evolved into a proto-lung, enabling these fish to spend longer and longer periods outside of the water. As there were no seagulls, pelicans, or other aerial carnivores to eat these fish, they developed the ability to flop, jump, and waddle their way onshore to eat the insects and plant life. The lobed fins and proto-lungs allowed the fittest fish to reproduce nearer to the land and spend more time above water. Over tens of millions of years, lobed fins developed into stumpy proto-legs, and the proto-lungs evolved into fully capable lungs.

Then, it finally happened.

Fishy in appearance, yet complete with primitive legs and the ability to breathe the fresh air, the first animal emerged from the water to live permanently on land. These animals resembled salamanders of today, and first crawled out of their ocean homes around four hundred million years ago. These early salamanders grew massive, likely from the higher oxygen content in the air thanks to billions of years of oxygenation by ocean-dwelling bacteria, and from the abundance of available food. The dinosaurs evolved out of these giant salamanders, starting with monsters like *Dimetrodon*. The dinosaurs ruled the earth for a staggering 165 million years. From this line came modern lizards, snakes, and crocodiles, hence the similarities in appearance.

The eukaryote branch of evolution that led to birds is closely related to the branch that created reptiles and dinosaurs. Paleontologists discovered many household-name dinosaurs, like *T. rex* and *Velociraptor*, likely had feathers protruding from their skin. Birds and dinosaurs also share the common characteristics of hollow bones, hooked claws, and a unique leg bone structure. In some sense, dinosaurs remain all around us today, as some of them evolved into the eighteen thousand species of birds found all over the globe.

The final major branch on the tree of life led to mammals, including our very own species of *Homo sapiens*. This branch connects through the reptilian, amphibian, and even fish branches. The mammalian branch, like every other part of the tree, ultimately traces its roots all the way back to the single-celled LUCA.

One of the most interesting stories within the mammalian branch is that of the whale, as these giants of the sea completed an evolutionary full circle of sorts. Fish once crawled out of the oceans and onto dry land. But many millions of years later, whales decided to crawl from the land back into the sea. The great-great-grandparent of the whale is known as *Ambulocetus*. *Ambulocetus* looks like a large mammal well adapted for swimming. The name *Ambulocetus* translates to "walking whale" as it displayed characteristics of both land-dwelling mammals and sea-dwelling swimmers. As this new animal spent more time underwater, it developed the ability to hold its breath for longer and longer periods of time. It developed webbed feet, like those of an otter, which, over time, went on to become fins. Finally, the animal took to the sea and never looked back.

Fast-forward a long time and the mammal began to look more like a dolphin of today. After more time, it evolved into the giant modern-day whale. Aquatic mammals like whales bear their young live, rather than in eggs, and require air to breathe at regular intervals. The process of evolution has yet to turn their lungs back into sea bladders and gills, though perhaps this development lies in their future.

Humanity, too, is part of the mammalian legacy. If we zoom

out far enough, we will find a common ancestor between *Homo sapiens* and every fungus, plant, and animal alive, as all of life stems from LUCA, sharing 20 to 98 percent of their DNA. As a whole, biologic life is quite literally one big family. In fact, we can see evidence of our evolutionary history within our own bodies. Our lungs may have been the swim bladders of fish in the distant past. Our fingernails may be the modern iteration of ancient mammalian claws. Our tailbone may be the vestige of an actual tail belonging to one of our distant ancestors. It's fascinating when you consider the implications.

As with all species, human evolution is an ongoing process, constantly progressing to the next phase. Our appendix is a good example of this. It may have served a very specific function for us at some point in our past, but no longer. Surgically removing this organ from our bodies doesn't significantly impact our lives or health. If this evolution continues, future generations of humans may be born with no appendix at all.

The Controversy of Life

The controversy of life remains a difficult one to reconcile. The theory of gradual evolution, apart from any work of God, is impossible for believers to accept. I understand this difficulty well, as it has also been the greatest area of struggle in my own mind. The dispute over how life happened has raged for millennia. Early forms of this argument were seen way back in the ancient Greek materialist philosophies of Democritus and Epicurus. The Roman poet Lucretius carried their concepts further with his argument that all of life is simply atoms moving in the void. Pure materialism, no God needed. These ideas have survived throughout the ages. Stoked by Charles Darwin in the nineteenth century, atheists hold strongly to similar arguments. Life is a whole and complete mechanism on its own. No God necessary.

When I read *On the Origin of Species*, I was struck by the sense that Darwin was recording his observations of the natural world as he encountered it, similar to the way Aristotle had on the island of Lesbos. I remember thinking, *I can't really fault a guy for just reporting what he sees*, and wondering why the religious community demonized him so severely. It wasn't until I read both sides of the argument in later years that I came to a sense of the issue at hand. While it is true Darwin started out simply recording what he saw in the natural world, the problem came when he later offered some conclusions on evolution that were not based on his observed evidence. An example of this is the assumption that macroevolution (think a big jump from dinosaur to bird) is true because you observe microevolution (adaptation within the same species) is true. He outlined these controversial conclusions in greater detail in his later book, *The Descent of Man*. The problems with evolutionary theory lie in the unproven conclusions and not Darwin's initial observations.

As humanity makes new scientific discoveries, our data clearly supports the theory that plants and animals adapt to their environments over many generations. We've known this for a long time in plant and animal husbandry, just as Darwin himself bred plants to attain specific characteristics over successive generations. In some ways, modern genetic modification of food and animals is an updated form of selective evolution. Darwin's assertion of *survival of the fittest* concurs with modern scientific observations. Beneficial biologic variations pass on to the next generation while the poorly equipped offspring die out. Most people, even those strongly opposed to modern science, can agree with the idea that a species becomes more suitable for their environment as the fittest survive to out-reproduce the others.

As we have said, the problem is not whether a species adapts over time (microevolution); rather, it is whether one species can change into an entirely new species (macroevolution), given enough time. Did the dinosaurs evolve into today's birds? Did a land-dwelling mammal really jump back into the ocean and evolve into the modern whale? It is easy, and fascinating, to see how Darwin's Galapagos finches evolved four different beaks from the varied food sources on four different islands, but can these same birds go on to evolve into an entirely new animal altogether? That is a much more challenging question.

THE FOSSIL PROBLEM

Mary Anning (1799–1847) made history at the young age of twelve when she discovered an ichthyosaur skeleton on the coastal cliffs of England. Mary went on to become a pioneer in the field of paleontology, though many of her findings were not officially recognized until after her death. In a time when most people believed in a literal interpretation of Genesis, Mary's finds challenged their beliefs that the earth was only thousands of years old. Her work, and that of generations of paleontologists that followed, have provided us with a "window to the past." Fossils have become one of the most fascinating forms of prehistoric knowledge that have also helped us rewrite our understanding of geological history.

That being said, one of evolution's biggest challenges remains the lack of evidence found in the fossil record, a problem Darwin himself foresaw in his own theory. In the fossil record, we simply don't see a significant number of *transitioning* fossils.

If every animal population is in constant flux, morphing always into something else as Darwin proposed, then the fossil record should be full of examples of those species caught in transition from one species to the next. Darwin was aware of this lack of fossil evidence and he hoped future excavations would discover more transitioning fossils to help bolster his theory. While scientists agree that the way fossilization works makes it an extremely rare occurrence in natural history, in the hundreds of years since Darwin, our new fossil finds seem to reveal a different story than gradual change over time.

In his 1991 book *Darwin on Trial*, Phillip Johnson looks at the theory of evolution from the objective stance of a lawyer. He presents what the scientific evidence of the last 150 years has discovered. The most convincing transitional fossils we have are the small dinosaur birds archaeopteryx and the fishy, salamander-like tetrapods whose four stumpy legs could pass for fins in transition.

The larger picture of the fossil record seems to tell a story other than gradual change over time. What we find in the record are periods lasting tens of millions of years where animals show very minimal changes. These long static periods are then followed by a mass extinction event that kills off 70–95 percent of all life. After the mass extinction there then follows an explosion of new lifeforms that make up the next static period lasting millions of years. New life, then a long period with no changes, then an extinction event, finally more new life. So far there have been five mass extinction events in Earth's history, which leads to an interesting thought experiment on whether the five mass extinctions might be the *nights* to Genesis's six *days* of creation.

Other problems exist as well for evolutionary theory. There are issues debated among scientists on whether evolution is possible at the molecular level and there are further issues debated among philosophers as to whether evolution is possible from a philosophical standpoint. Fr. Chad Ripperger thoroughly presents the arguments from philosophy in his book *The Metaphysics of Evolution*. One of his main points originates from the basic philosophical principle that a more complex being cannot come from a less complex being.

FOUR OPTIONS

In the ongoing debate between faith and science, we are left with roughly four options of how life originated and developed. The first is by completely natural processes without any intervention by God. The second is by natural processes that God put into motion, often referred to as *theistic evolution* or *intelligent design*. Third comes creation by God all at once, or in a relatively short period, like the seven days described in Genesis (some interpret these verses of Scripture more literally than others). Fourth is the idea of *ongoing* or *continuous creation*, or the belief that God continues creating new life long after the beginning of the world.

I think it is important to highlight here that both theologians and scientists are, for the most part, seeking the truth of how things happened. Believers cannot accept the first option of natural processes apart from God's hand, but they also have a difficult time responding to the findings of modern science with an explanation that addresses the geologic and biologic history we find in the world. Those faithful to science alone, on the other hand, cannot accept literal versions of the Genesis story, but science apart from God has real challenges explaining why the Big Bang and the miracle of life happened at all, where matter and energy came from, and why it all appears directed or guided.

For myself, it really doesn't matter which one of the options is correct as long as it includes the data we know from science and recognizes a Creator. The reality is that we just don't have all the pieces collected to form a final conclusion—and that's okay; the mystery is still unfolding before our eyes. The wonder, for me, lies in each new scientific discovery of how the story of life happened. In recent years, I'm leaning toward creation through intelligent design that includes evolutionary processes as my preferred synthesis of faith and science. It offers a range of logical possibilities for the origin of life while also recognizing God's creative miracles and faithful preservation of the universe at every moment. It allows science to be its own source of revelation as we encounter more of the world and its history. At the same time, this synthesis maintains the necessity of Aristotle's Unmoved Mover as the First Cause of all things.

Consider that God created life on Earth through the natural *and* miraculous process of chemical evolution. Then, after these humble beginnings, He directed some form of evolution to take hold. Over billions of years, simple, single-celled organisms evolved into the diversity of living things we encounter in the world today. If this is indeed how it went, then perhaps God imprinted His image on life the same way He imprinted it on the universe.

God's Image in Life

LIFE WAS ONE

If the first moment of the Big Bang displayed oneness for the universe, then LUCA, the last universal common ancestor, similarly displayed unity for all of life. LUCA were tiny, single-celled organisms containing within them the potential to become every living thing. The single-celled ancestor of life was, like God, indivisible. Could you cut it in half with the finest of modern instruments? Sure. But it was indivisible in a different sense. To divide LUCA in any way would mean a destruction of the life within. It was indivisible from the perspective that if anything was removed from its simplicity, it would no longer be *alive*.

The analogy here is perhaps not as clearly seen as in the first moment of time; however, it remains true to the concept of God's oneness. In God, all things are perfectly one. He has no parts or physical body, and therefore there is nothing you could divide out even if you wanted to. The first cells are physical matter, and are therefore able to be divided; however, not without forfeiting the life within. In this way, God shows His oneness in the beginning of life.

The physical world, being bound by time, must move through time. Life changes and evolves away from this original oneness, but at its beginning it resembles the oneness of God. He communicates His unity through the simple, single cells living unobserved for billions of years in the waters of the primordial oceans. Inconspicuous though they were, they carried within them a near-infinite potential to become.

LIFE DISPLAYS INFINITY

After God's oneness, we note how life displays the attribute of God's infinity. Like the edges of the universe forever chasing infinite size, life possesses a similar quality in its near-infinite potential to evolve and change. From the single-celled bacteria to the branches in the tree of life, the living diversity we see all around us today is simply stunning. There is so much life and so much diversity. Bacteria, archaea, plants, animals, birds, insects, humans—and thousands of variations within each group. One very large family indeed.

Pure evolutionists claim random processes caused the differences we see in the animal kingdom. Perhaps we could look at it from a different perspective, however. When dealing with infinite possibilities, the route actually taken will appear random. Life could evolve in any direction, but it does so according to the environment and stressors Earth sets before it. If life evolved on another planet, with a completely different temperature, pressure, atmosphere, and so on, then it would undoubtedly look much different than it does here on ours.

Andy Weir's science fiction novel *Project Hail Mary* does a great job illustrating what an encounter with alien life from a vastly different planet might look like.[9] In the story, an astronaut tasked with saving Earth from a dying sun travels light-years away to study why a star, similar to our sun, is not dying from the same disease. When he arrives, he meets an alien species there on the very same mission, to save their own dying sun. The creature he encounters looks like a large five-legged spider that evolved on a planet with much higher temperatures, higher pressures, and less light than on Earth. Because of these conditions, the aliens evolved strong, mineral-like exoskeletons and a communication system based on sound and echolocation instead of sight. It is a fascinating exploration into the real possibilities of evolution under different conditions than ours. It also helps illustrate how the apparent randomness of evolution can be viewed as the particular, directed route taken through a near-infinite number of possibilities. What appears naturally random from our view may actually be directed by God at a level we cannot access through empirical science.

Life is immensely diverse. It contains the potential to evolve in endless ways, though it will only ever actualize a tiny amount of that potential no matter how many planets have life on them. The longer life lives on our planet, the more time it has to grow toward increasing diversity. The more diverse life becomes, the more it represents the infinity of God. Life begins resembling the oneness of God and ends in pursuit of the infinity of God, much like the universe does on a larger scale.

LIFE DISPLAYS ETERNITY

Think about this for a moment—the first single-celled bacteria likely emerged around four billion years ago. The earth itself is four and a half billion years old, which means life began relatively soon after the planet's formation. For a period of two to three billion years, single-celled organisms were all that existed. That is a long time of not much else happening. It wasn't until around seven hundred million years ago that multicellular life first emerged onto the scene. Since that time, life has been on a tear of growth and development.

Here again, the analogies of God's attributes are for us. Humanity is the only known being in the universe capable of seeing the analogies, receiving them, and understanding them. The extensive period of four billion years is much larger than our minds can comprehend. Day after day after endless day, a billion years becomes just a big number without any personal reference to back it up. However, it can be seen as an image of eternity. God takes His time with what He creates; there is no rush.

When we think back on the length of time it takes for life to evolve, it reveals that God was present in every moment of the process just as He is present now. During this multibillion-year expanse of time passing by while life evolves, God did not change at all. He was present in full actuality just as He is now—the same at every moment: 13.8 billion years ago, four billion years ago, yesterday, today, and forever.

LIFE IS UNKNOWABLE

The attribute of God's unknowability can be seen most distinctly at life's origin. The analogy is simply this: To date, we are still unable to create life in a lab. The miracle of life through abiogenesis is, for some unknown reason, not replicable. The creation of a living thing from nonliving things remains a mystery to us just as God's own essence remains a mystery.

In *Darwin on Trial*, Phillip Johnson adds to this mystery, saying the odds of life self-assembling through abiogenesis are absurdly low. He writes the following:

> The simplest organism capable of independent life, the prokaryote bacterial cell, is a masterpiece of miniaturized complexity which makes a spaceship seem rather low-tech. Even if one assumes that something much simpler than a bacterial cell might suffice to start Darwinist evolution on its way—a DNA or RNA macromolecule, for example—the possibility that such a complex entity could assemble itself by chance is still fantastically unlikely, even if billions of years had been available . . . a metaphor by Fred Hoyle has become famous because it vividly conveys the magnitude of the problem: that a living organism emerged by chance from a prebiotic soup is about as likely as that "a

tornado sweeping through a junkyard might assemble a Boeing 747 from the materials therein."[10]

It is an interesting conundrum, seeing as we have a decent idea of the composition of the primordial atmosphere. By now, we should have been able to create a living cell in some modern version of the Miller-Urey experiment, yet we have failed to do so. Miller and Urey tried unsuccessfully to re-create life in 1952, with others attempting similar failed experiments in the decades following. Will we get there eventually? Perhaps. For now, however, the exact science that lies behind the miracle of life remains veiled from our knowledge, just as the comprehension of God's essence remains similarly veiled from our sight.

CHAPTER 8

The Human Mind

"People go abroad to wonder at the heights of mountains, at the huge waves of the sea, at the vast compass of the ocean, at the circular motions of the stars, and they pass by themselves without wondering."

—Augustine

Fable

As you and Sophia stand on the shores of the ancient sea gazing out at the waters, she notices a look of concern on your face.

"What's the matter?" she asks.

"Well, it's fascinating to think that all of life came from the same place out there in the ocean. I mean, it's amazing that all living things are related to one another like that.... But"—you pause for a moment, searching for the right words, then continue—"I've always thought humanity was unique in some way, and not just another one of the animals."

"Ah, yes, an excellent point," she replies. "I would agree with you; humanity is very special indeed. You are the animals set apart to bear the Image. Only humanity carries within it the mark of the Creator, like no other animal ever has before or ever will. In fact, you are displaying that image right here in our discussion. It can be seen in the great conversation of Plato and Aristotle that's endured for thousands of years. And it shows itself anywhere the human mind is at work contemplating higher realities."

"Interesting," you say. "Please, tell me more . . ."

A Bridge Between Two Worlds

Humanity stands as a bridge between two worlds. On the one hand, our bodies are participants in the long history of life's evolution on Earth. On the other hand, we are members of a much larger unseen world that's invisible to scientific detection. This is the nonphysical world that includes complex rational thought; mathematics; values and virtues; transcendental concepts like truth, beauty, and goodness; and the awareness of God.

This entrance into the world of immaterial things is what sets humanity distinctly apart from the other animals. Why have we been granted access to this depth of meaning when no other animal seems to have developed the same capacity? Are we simply the latest step in the evolutionary chain or is there something more to us, a deeper element, one that allows us to participate in this unseen world?

In this chapter, we will consider the idea that God placed a unique human soul into the evolutionary line of primates. It would have happened in a way similar to the first living cells that sprang from nonliving matter—on an ordinary day like so many others. When the form of humanity's body had reached fulfillment over millions of years, God placed within it the animating principal of an immortal, rational soul. It is this specific attribute that endows us today with the ability to see into the invisible world of higher things.

Think about the idea for a moment—God placed a soul into the human animal at the proper time. If this is true, then two related conclusions might also be true. The first is seeing humanity as the end-in-mind and the goal (telos) of evolution. When God began the process of evolution with just single cells, it was humanity He had in mind as the end goal. The second conclusion is that we should be able to see major changes in the archaeological record brought about by such an addition to the animal line. If an animal is endowed with an immortal soul, where before it had none, then we ought to see very big differences in the way this animal lived and acted. Interestingly, that is exactly what we find in the archaeology of ancient humanity.

A Brief History of Humanity

Biologically speaking, modern humans belong to the species of primates known as *Homo sapiens*, meaning "wise man." Our oldest fossil records, as of this writing, date back around three hundred thousand years to a recently uncovered Moroccan mine. The Moroccan remains reveal a small group of *Homo sapiens* living in a cave, hunting gazelle with stone-tipped spears. These cave-dwelling people were similar to humans of today except for slightly elongated skulls and brains. Before this find, the oldest known fossils of *Homo sapiens* were found thousands of miles away in Ethiopia, dating back around two hundred thousand years. These finds act as reminders that humanity, as a species, has been here for quite a while.

The larger archaeological picture reveals another interesting fact: *Homo sapiens* were not alone. Digs from all over have found at least eight *Homo* species who lived as contemporaries to *Homo sapiens* in various parts of the world and in various time periods. There were many variations of prehumans living in differing geographical regions, each group specifically suited for their environment thanks to the processes of genetic variation, natural selection, and cooperation.

Homo neanderthalensis, for example, was one contemporary of *Homo sapiens*. *Homo neanderthalensis*, more commonly referred to as the Neanderthals, lived in the areas where Europe and Central Asia now stand. These early prehumans were shorter and stockier than *Homo sapiens* and were well adapted to living in the colder northern climates. The Neanderthals had a brain size comparable to ours and were known to perform many of the same daily functions that *Homo sapiens* did. Archaeology reveals they were skilled at hunting, they made clothing, they used sophisticated tools, and they may have even buried their dead in marked graves. Other close relatives to our forefathers included the *Homo naledi* of South Africa and the *Homo heidelbergensis* of Europe.

The *Homo* branch of the evolutionary tree traces back to around six million years, when the first bipedal hominids emerged out of the primate group. For context, hominin refers to humans and their direct ancestors while hominid is a broader classification that includes all hominins as well as great apes. These early hominids did not yet boast the large skull and brain that we humans enjoy today. In fact, their brains were around 35 percent the size of ours. Nevertheless, they were the first primates to stand up on two feet and walk upright.

Australopithecus was the first recognizable genus to solidify out of these prehuman primates and they did so around four million years ago, in southern Africa. If observed, these prehumans would have oddly resembled both the primates from which they came, as well as the hominins they would evolve to become. They most likely began living up in the trees, eating the plentiful vegetation, and then later, over millions of years, developed the ability to walk on two legs, spending more and more time on the ground hunting prey.

In 1974, Donald Johnson and Tom Gray of the Cleveland Museum of Natural History discovered ancient remains of an early hominin at the site of Hadar, Ethiopia. During the celebration of their find, the song "Lucy in the Sky with Diamonds" was playing on the radio, so they affectionately gave the female remains the name Lucy. Lucy has been dated to around 3.1 million years old and is considered an important find because she displays the evolutionary transition from ape to hominin. Lucy stood about three feet, seven inches tall and weighed around sixty pounds.[1] She had the appearance and skull shape similar to that of a chimpanzee, but her pelvis and leg bones were more like those of modern humans. Critics of the Lucy find argue that only small amounts of bone were found—not nearly enough evidence to draw the kinds of evolutionary conclusions many proposed. Still, the evolutionary theory of ape to hominin to *Homo sapiens* remains strong in the scientific community.

What's interesting about the evolution of the human species is the fact that our brain size continued to grow so large. There doesn't seem to be a clear survival advantage to having an oversized brain, as it uses a large percentage of the body's energy supply even while at rest. Apes have smaller brains, for instance, but they are much stronger than we are and could easily win in a battle for territory. Intelligence, then, must be the evolutionary advantage a larger brain gives us.

Around seventy thousand years ago, we see a definitive change within the *Homo* species that altered the course of the world forever. There isn't a clear scientific explanation as to why this change occurred, but the results it brought about were irreversible. For hundreds of thousands of years, *Homo sapiens* were happy to live in their own areas, sometimes alongside other *Homo* species and other times alone. Then, for some unknown reason, *Homo sapiens* began a mass migration out of Africa and into the surrounding world.

In his book titled *Sapiens*, historian Yuval Noah Harari writes, "What then drove forward the evolution of the massive human brain during those 2 million years? Frankly, we don't know."[2] Harari observes that what set *Homo sapiens* apart from the rest of their counterparts was their ability to work together. *Homo sapiens* gained the special ability to communicate en masse and, in doing so, could coordinate larger group activities. This new skill, combined with their mass migration out of Africa, allowed for their civilization to grow in both size and complexity.

Oddly, whenever *Homo sapiens* invaded the lands of other *Homo* groups during their migration, the other species eventually thinned and died out. Scientists argue this may have been due to competition for food, diseases brought in by the migrating *Homo sapiens*, or from ancient forms of war or genocide. The extinctions were not always immediate and sometimes took hundreds or thousands of years to complete. Still, we find the same conclusion playing out time and again—whenever *Homo sapiens* entered a new territory, the other species of *Homo* would either die out or move on. Consequently, *Homo sapiens* were left alone to use the native resources as they pleased and proliferate further in population.

Aside from the newfound ability to communicate and collaborate, other significant changes occurred within *Homo sapiens* never before seen in the animal kingdom. These changes clearly displayed the new, higher dimension now present within the human animal. Namely, the ability to recognize the unseen world distinct from the physical one.

We see these new abilities in the archaeological record in the form of worship and the practice of art. It is difficult to pinpoint the exact time when these changes entered the *Homo sapiens* line, as archaeological finds of this age are extremely scarce. Even so, there is plenty of evidence that suggests before seventy thousand to three hundred thousand years ago, there was no worship or art practiced in the animal kingdom, whereas after this period, artifacts of both worship and art are nearly always found alongside human remains.

WORSHIP AS UNIQUELY HUMAN

It seems clear that something rather significant occurred in our history that allowed ancient humans to realize the presence of the divine among them. We became aware of a higher being existing with us in the world, one that held more power than ourselves and so deserved to be venerated and/or feared. Our natural response to such a presence showed up in the form of worship. Divine worship has been a staple of human history for so long that we take for granted the much longer expanse of time when the animal kingdom performed no such thing. In nearly every ancient human culture, civilization, clan, or society, there almost always exists the worship of some God, gods, great spirit, or deity.

One of the earliest examples we have of this new phenomenon of worship was found in the Tsodilo Hills of Botswana. There, archaeologists uncovered a unique python-shaped rock carving on a cave wall. Other artifacts and tools in the cave date it back to around seventy thousand years. No human settlement has been found near the area, which led researchers to postulate this might be one of the oldest known sites made specifically for worship and veneration. While others disagree with this interpretation, the indigenous Bushmen in the area today still hold beliefs that the Tsodilo Hills are sacred to the gods.

In its earliest forms, evidence of worship began with ceremonial burial practices and the veneration of animals or local land formations. The example of the Tsodilo Hills shows this expression of divinity attributed to natural things—the python-shaped rock. Jacques Cauvin suggests that religion was truly born a bit later, in the Neolithic era, or Stone Age (10,000 BC), in what he calls the "Revolution of the Symbols."[3] Archaeological finds from the Neolithic era show several different symbols, including those of women goddesses, gods in the form of bulls, and pictures of half-animal, half-humans revealing early shamanistic practices. Symbols found throughout human history in and around sacred sites and burial lands reveal humanity's new awareness of the sacred other.

Regardless of how or when it started, we know that worship and religion have found expression only within the *Homo sapiens* species. The history of religion has taken on a long and winding evolution of its own, much like the evolution of life on Earth. The following timeline offers a quick summary of humanity's development of worship:

1. 200,000 BC   *Homo naledi* burial grounds in South Africa

2. 100,000 BC   Rising Star burial grounds in the Middle East

3. 70,000 BC   The Tsodilo Hills reveal possible animal and land formation veneration

4. 40,000 BC   The earliest known cremation of human remains near Lake Mungo in Australia

5. 38,000 BC   The oldest known animal-shaped figurine is made and later interpreted to have anthropomorphic properties resembling a local deity

6. 9100 BC   Gobekli Tepe in modern-day Turkey is later confirmed as one of the oldest human-made sites used for worship

7. 7500 BC   The settlement of Catalhoyuk in modern-day Turkey develops as a spiritual center where numerous clay figurines of phallic and feminine symbols were later found

8. 3100 BC   Stonehenge in England is built

9. 3000 BC   Sumerian Cuneiform emerges, allowing the first codification of beliefs and the first written stories of creation; before this time all religion was passed down through oral tradition

10.	2560 BC	The Great Pyramid of Giza is completed in Egypt; Egyptian religious texts were also created around this time
11.	2100 BC	The Sumerian Epic of Gilgamesh is completed
12.	1700 BC	The oldest of the Hindu Vegas, the Rig Veda, is written
13.	1200 BC	The Upanishads (Vedic Texts) are composed containing the basic building blocks of Hinduism and later Buddhism
14.	1200 BC	The Greek gods appear on the scene
15.	600 BC	The Jewish Torah is written (though its history began much earlier) containing the building blocks for Judaism and later Christianity and Islam
16.	551 BC	Confucius, founder of Confucianism, is born
17.	480 BC	Gautama Buddha, founder of Buddhism, is born
18.	399 BC	Socrates is tried and found guilty in Athens for corrupting the youth
19.	0	Jesus of Nazareth is born
20.	405 AD	St. Jerome completes the Latin Vulgate, the first translation of the Bible

21.	570 AD	The Prophet Muhammad, founder of Islam, is born
22.	632 AD	The compilation of the Qur'an begins
23.	1054 AD	The Great Schism between the Roman Catholic and Eastern Orthodox Churches occurs
24.	1517 AD	Martin Luther posts his Ninety-Five Theses and the Protestant Reformation begins, becoming the foundation for the many Protestant groups we see today
25.	1823 AD	The Mormon Prophet, Joseph Smith, writes the Book of Mormon and founds the Church of Latter-day Saints
26.	1954 AD	The Church of Scientology is founded by L. Ron Hubbard

Today we have a dizzying array of religions as well as endless expressions of worship. Humanity continues to venerate one God, many gods, sacred people, sacred animals, sacred land formations, the Universe, and almost anything to which it can attribute divine characteristics. The important point here is not which form of worship is the correct form, but rather that worship of any sort arrived on the scene where before it had never existed. It has become a part of humanity that has never left us. There is something special and particularly unique within us that recognizes the presence of God that no other animal possesses.

ART AS UNIQUELY HUMAN

The second new ability introduced into the world of *Homo sapiens* was the practice of art, including music. As with worship, art and music are new, uniquely human actions seen for the first time after the period ranging from seventy thousand to three hundred thousand years ago. Musical sounds in the form of birdsong and the like undoubtedly existed within the animal kingdom before this time; however, *Homo sapiens* introduced its practice with a wholly new purpose. While animals use musical sounds for specific utilities, for example, to attract mates or warn of nearby dangers, humanity performs music as an art form. *Homo sapiens* use music and dance in celebration of the beauty of life and the world around them. It springs from a direct response of our ability to see the deeper meaning written into the universe.

These quotes from various points in history help highlight the difference between this new celebratory music and the older animal sounds:

> "Music is a moral law. It gives a soul to the universe, wings to the mind, flight to the imagination and charm and gaiety to life and to everything." —Plato

> "Music is the language of the soul." —Saint Cecilia

> "Music is the voice that tells us that the human race is greater than it knows." —Napoleon

> "The purpose of music is to uplift the soul and bring joy to the heart." —Beethoven

"Music expresses that which cannot be said and on which it is impossible to be silent." —Victor Hugo

"If I had my life to live over again, I would have made a rule to read some poetry and listen to some music at least once every week." —Charles Darwin

"Music is the universal language . . . it brings people closer together." —Ella Fitzgerald

From these quotes and countless like them, the depth of humanity's appreciation for music highlights the stark difference between us and the other animals—depth, meaning, and insight into the higher things of life, a new ability to see directly into the world of God.

Art and music have been used throughout history to communicate stories, lore, and emotion. At their core, however, they are actions done for the sake of celebration and appreciation of the beauty around us. Since their entrance onto the scene many thousands of years ago, music and art, as with worship, have been found in every human civilization archaeology has uncovered, with few exceptions.

The Caves of Lascaux

Humanity recognizes intuitively that art is a worthwhile pursuit—a sacred one, even. On September 12, 1940, eighteen-year-old Marcel Ravidat was out exploring the countryside near his hometown of Montignac, France, along with his dog, Robot.[4] As they walked along, the boy noticed an old pine tree had fallen over, revealing a tunnel in the ground. As dogs do, Robot ran straight into the hole, with the adventurous teenager climbing in after him. At first, Marcel thought he had stumbled upon the cave of a lost treasure from local legend. Instead, he had stumbled upon another sort of treasure—arguably of much greater value.

Realizing he hadn't brought the proper excavation tools along, Marcel returned to town to recruit three of his friends. Four days later, the teens made their way back to the site and dug further into the cave. Using a makeshift lamp, they illuminated the darkness to discover the ancient cave paintings of Lascaux, France. The paintings turned out to be some of the oldest and most well-preserved art in ancient history, dating back seventeen to twenty thousand years.

The cave walls were covered in masterful strokes of black, red, and yellow, displaying images of bison, horses, birds, and deer. The four boys agreed they had found something very special and decided to keep it a secret. They worried about careless people hearing about the cave and destroying its artwork. Eventually, the boys confided in a local historian who agreed they should guard the paintings at all costs.

Taking it as a sacred duty, the four teens made a pact to set up camp outside the entrance to Lascaux and guard their treasure around the clock. One of the boys, Jacques Marsal, only fourteen at the time, camped out in front of the cave throughout the notably harsh winter of 1940–41. Young Jacques considered his duty so solemn, in fact, he went on to spend the remainder of his life as a warden of the Lascaux caves, up until his death in 1989.

The art the boys found in the caves was special and they knew it instinctively, an indication that art speaks to the deeper sense in us. The insightful English author G.K. Chesterton discussed the phenomena of ancient cave art at length in his work *The Everlasting*

Man. Writing on the effect cave art would have on a modern boy encountering it for the first time, he says the following:

> It must surely strike him as strange that men so remote from him should be so near, and that beasts so near to him should be so remote. To his simplicity it must seem at least odd that he could not find any trace of the beginning of any arts among any animals. That is the simplest lesson to learn in the cavern of the coloured pictures; only it is too simple to be learnt. It is the simple truth that man does differ from the brutes in kind and not in degree; and the proof of it is here; that it sounds like a truism to say that the most primitive man drew a picture of a monkey and that it sounds like a joke to say that the most intelligent monkey drew a picture of a man. Something of division and disproportion has appeared; and it is unique. Art is the signature of man.[5]

The Rational Soul

Homo sapiens stand out from the evolutionary animal line in a distinct way. Animal life has somehow gained access to the unseen world of rationality for the first time and a new dimension to our existence has been added in. *Homo sapiens* now have cognition, consciousness, and awareness of higher realities. We recognize the existence of something greater than ourselves present in the world and we respond in worship. Humanity also sees that the world can be a beautiful place worthy of celebration through art and music. Something is different about the animal kingdom now; something new has been born. But what exactly is this new dimension inside of *Homo sapiens*?

Aristotle described the human person as a *rational animal*. In his work *The Nichomachean Ethics*, he observed that humanity contains within it the nutritive power of plants to grow, the propulsive elements of animals to move about freely, and a new, distinctive element that he called the *rational principle*. This rational principle is what makes humans human and no longer simply one of the animals. The rational principle is what gives us self-knowledge, the ability for complex thought, an understanding of mathematics, and the power of imagination. It is also what moves us to bow down in worship of God and create works of beauty through art and music.

OUR MINDS AS A BLANK SLATE

The earliest known writing tablets were found written in Sumerian and date back to around 3200 BC. These tablets were made of clay and later of wax. They were used to record local laws and business transactions of the time. To write on the tablets, the author would use a stylus made of reed to impress letters into the clay. To erase the tablet, the user would simply wet the clay and then smooth it out until it was returned to a blank surface once again.

Philosophers later referred to this writing method as an example of how humanity's rational principle works. The term *tabula rasa* translates to "blank slate" and expresses the state of the rational mind at rest. The human mind, like the clay writing tablet, is a blank slate waiting to be impressed upon with new ideas. Aristotle was one of the earliest philosophers to teach this concept. In *De Anima* Book 3, Part 4, he writes, "Mind is in a sense potentially whatever is thinkable, though actually it is nothing until it has thought. What it thinks must be in it just as characters may be said to be on a writing-tablet on which as yet nothing stands written: this is exactly what happens with mind."[6] He goes on to emphasize the near-infinite potential of the human mind to think of almost anything we put into it. The mind's rational principle stands ready to take on whatever ideas we want to consider. The possibilities are endless.

The Islamic philosopher Avicenna added to Aristotle's thought in the eleventh century, writing, "The human intellect at birth resembles a tabula rasa, a pure potentiality that is actualized through education and comes to know."[7] Avicenna believed that the human mind, the rational principle, is specifically our unique power to know. Every one of us has this same blank slate within, ready to be imprinted with any number of new ideas.

John Locke continued this concept of the mind as a blank slate in the late 1600s. Locke believed that when we are born, our minds arrive complete, but empty of any knowledge. We have the ability to learn anything, but we do not arrive with any innate, prior knowledge preloaded. We have been given a special capacity that stands ready to be filled up throughout our lifetimes and we actualize that potential through experiences and learning.

For Locke, the human mind takes in knowledge through a variety of ways, including the five senses, human experience, and self-reflection. In his *Essay Concerning Human Understanding*, Locke writes, "Let us then suppose the mind to be, as we say, white paper void of all characters, without any ideas. How comes it to be furnished? Whence comes it by that vast store which the busy and boundless fancy of man has painted on it with an almost endless variety? Whence has it all the materials of reason and knowledge? To this I answer, in one word, from experience."[8] On a side note, notice the tech upgrade from clay tablets to paper. Here, Locke argues that *experience* is how we gain knowledge. It is not something innate to us when born, though he recognizes—and with some sense of wonder—the infinite and "almost endless variety" of ideas that our minds can create.

Human thinking flows from a state of tabula rasa toward a near-infinite complexity of ideas. In the act of thinking, we begin with a simple, blank mind ready to take on new concepts—our minds are the clay tablets ready for imprinting. When we call to mind an idea, or learn something new, our mind grows in complexity. Because we can store previously learned information as memory, this gives us the ability to wipe the slate clean once more and reset our minds back to the state of the tabula rasa, ready to take on more new ideas. Over the course of a lifetime, the stored memories act as a reference library from which to draw on when contemplating new things. In this way, our thoughts grow deeper and increasingly complex. If we continue in the pursuit of learning, our knowledge can compound over the course of our lives like a well-funded IRA.

IDEAS

Ideas have a staying power about them. They can take on a life of their own and grow in sophistication over many generations of human lives. Ideas are timeless in that way. As long as there are minds to pass on the ideas and new minds to receive them, they live on through the years long after their originators are gone.

The development of the rational image of God discussed in Part I is an excellent example of the timelessness of ideas. From Plato and Aristotle to the synthesizers of the major monotheistic faiths, the ideas surrounding God's essence grew and developed over many centuries. Plato's idea of universal forms, for instance, continues to be carried and developed in the minds of humanity today. Each new mind learning the knowledge passed on from their teacher, down through the generations, evolving the original body of thought by adding new insights of their own along the way.

Through this progressive nature of human knowledge, ideas grow in complexity over time, developing in endless new ways, similar to the evolutionary branches on the tree of life. Take the phenomenon of money, for example. When early humans needed something of value, they used the barter system to trade with tribes from other areas—a trade of two objects similar in value. The barter system works only so well, however, as it can be difficult to exactly match the value of a bow and arrow to the value of a sparkling gemstone. Furthermore, the issue of traveling with items of value and trading in large quantities provides its own challenges.

Eventually, humanity needed an agreed-upon store of value to trade among themselves. Enter money. Money has taken many forms over time and across cultures: shiny cowrie shells, large stones, leather squares, metal coins, paper notes, and now digital cryptocurrencies stored in computer algorithms. In every instance, one group of people makes a collaborative agreement among themselves that this particular object will have this particular value. Money provides a standardized barter system allowing for easier cross-cultural exchanges.

Fast-forward to the modern day and the complexity of our monetary system is staggering. We now boast global markets where people buy and sell small pieces of equity ownership in large corporations in the form of stocks. We can then trade these pieces of ownership back and forth for monetary value based on an agreed-upon market price that changes by the second according to pre-programmed market algorithms.

Growing further in complexity is the world of monetary derivatives. We can buy and sell a bet on whether a specific stock will trend up or down over a specified time period. Add leverage in the form of credit from the bank to that bet and we can now borrow money from someone else to place massive bets on these market fluctuations. The reality of it can be overwhelming. And it's all based on agreed-upon rules in the mathematical-financial world of unseen ideas. Once set in motion, the money markets run on by themselves, regardless if one investor takes a vacation and ceases to think about it for a day.

BRAIN AND SOUL TOGETHER

The unique human mind can be viewed as a combination of the brain organ and the powers of the rational soul. One requires the other and vice versa. We are as fully dependent on our physical bodies as we are on the animating principle within to access the world of higher things. You can see this relationship functioning when you look at the development of a child. In children, the human spark is visible and alive, sometimes even more so than in adults. Children learn by soaking in the world around them like sponges in search of wonder. As a child grows and their brain matures, they gain an increased ability to know the unseen world around them. Their thinking evolves in complexity over the years, revealing that the human rational principle is intimately tied to the physical body as much as it is the soul within.

The human mind is an anomaly within the animal kingdom. In terms of rationality, we are light-years ahead of even the second-smartest animal. Many in the world of science argue our powers of rationality are simply the result of having a larger brain or from having a larger brain-to-body-weight ratio. The problem here is there are more than a few animals who beat humans in both categories. The sperm whale, for instance, crushes us in overall brain weight, coming in at an impressive seventeen pounds compared to our relatively small three pounds. As for brain-to-body-weight ratio, the tiny shrew is way ahead of humans with a ratio of 10 percent compared to our 2 percent.[9]

The best argument for biology alone as the sole cause of our rationality must be the argument of higher complexity in brain structure. We as humans hold the title for the largest complex structures within our brains. Our neocortex and prefrontal cortex, the areas responsible for higher-order functioning and decision-making, are particularly more developed in humans than in other animals. We know that our rational powers are indeed tied to the organ of the brain. This becomes obvious in the unfortunate event of a brain injury where brain damage is sustained. When the brain organ is damaged, the powers of rationality greatly diminish.

Could it be possible that the greater complexity of our brain structure alone is responsible for the enormous chasm between our rational capabilities compared to every other animal's? Perhaps. For me, however, our slightly more complex brain structure doesn't adequately answer the question of why we are so vastly advanced in our powers of thought. A relatively more complex brain just doesn't add up to an infinitely more powerful rational capacity.

Ancient philosophy asserted the existence of an immortal soul in humanity with the argument known as *like recognizes like*. The principle says, if you have the ability to recognize timeless things like truth, beauty, goodness, and mathematics, then there must logically be something within you that has the equivalent characteristic. The timeless in you recognizes the timeless in other things. Creatures without this special characteristic are completely unaware of the timeless unseen world around them. If God placed a rational soul into humanity at the proper time along the evolutionary line, perhaps His image can be seen written into us in the same way He wrote it into the universe and into life.

God's Image in the Human Mind

The Creation of Adam by Renaissance painter Michelangelo is one of the most famous religious works in Western history. The painting depicts God the Father in human form reaching out to touch the finger of Adam. While Adam is lying leisurely on the ground, God is actively moving toward him on a cloud of angels in the creative act that breathes life into man.

What's fascinating about the image, among so many things, is the shape of the pink cloud surrounding God the Father. Upon closer inspection, the cloud is painted in the exact same shape as the human brain. The color matches, too. Michelangelo was well educated in anatomy as well as theology, and he used that knowledge to portray a deeper meaning in his art. What we are left with is the revelation that God placed the gift of his *mind* into the human creature. It is in our rational mind that we bear the image of God most clearly. While the Big Bang and life bear God's image in the physical realm, the human mind bears it in a nonphysical way. Because of this, it may be harder to tease out the image of God within; however, it may also be the closest representation of the divine we can find.

THE HUMAN MIND IS ONE

The human mind at rest may be the closest analogy of God's oneness in the entire universe. Aristotle says the mind at rest is a tabula rasa, blank and empty, waiting to be written upon. There are no divisions in the resting mind, nothing to separate out from something else, just a near-infinite capacity to think of whatever we put into it.

In those rare moments when we're able to calm our minds from their ceaseless streams of thought and truly come to rest, there is often a peace that accompanies the mental stillness. It is in these quieter moments that we are able to catch a glimpse into the unity of our own minds. Completely at rest and perfectly one.

The mind at rest exists in a near-infinite potential state, waiting to be actualized. In many ways, the resting mind resembles the first moment of the Big Bang and the first cells of life. All three are simple and indivisible. All three are unities containing endless potential to become. The mind at rest, in a real way, reveals the image of God's divine oneness.

THE HUMAN MIND DISPLAYS INFINITY

Once the mind begins to actualize its resting potential, it moves forward, thinking in an endless variety of complexities. Like regular mental Big Bangs, every time we begin a new thought process, we venture out toward an infinite diversity of thoughts.

Take a moment to rest your mind and think of nothing. From

this point, now think of a small, simple white house. Think of that house in every color of the rainbow. Now think of it as a one-story, two-story, three-story house and so on. Add stripes to the exterior and then polka dots. Add trees next to the house, and then color them any way you want—add three, four, five, however many you want. The thought experiment could go on like this forever; it is literally endless. Whether we're analyzing empirical data and drawing interpretative conclusions or imagining entire worlds that we put to paper in fictional works, the mind's bounds seem limitless.

The human mind is one of the most powerful tools in the world. Its potential to think, strategize, and create is almost infinite. In this way, the mind at work resembles the infinity of God. Within the human mind, as within the size of the universe and the diversity of life, infinity is a potential never to be reached. Still, the image is there, shining forth when we use our minds with the rational power infused into us.

THE HUMAN MIND DISPLAYS ETERNITY

Are our minds eternal? Well, each of us had a beginning, but our rational souls may not have an end. Christianity teaches that only God is eternal, having no beginning and no end. But the human soul is said to be immortal—having a beginning but not having an end. The Christian view is that our soul lives on after death, awaiting the resurrection of the body when Jesus Christ comes again. Our soul is made to be one with our physical bodies; only in death do they separate—but only for a time. Eventually we will be reunited as body and soul forever. In that way, our immortality bears some resemblance to the eternity of God.

As previously discussed, ideas themselves convey another image of the eternal. Great ideas, ones passed down from generation to generation, grow and develop within the minds of humanity long after their originators have passed on. The ideas live for centuries and remain in the minds of people for many generations.

Stephen Covey's timeless book *The Seven Habits of Highly Effective People* comes to mind here. Covey's book lays out seven proven habits for success that have shown true over many generations and in multiple cultures of the world. The principles underlying the habits are real and lasting. Not only are they timeless by being passed on from one mind to the next through the centuries, but even if forgotten for years by everyone, they remain just as real, ready to be rediscovered by future minds. One can see how ideas and concepts like these have an eternal quality about them, just like the human mind that knows them.

THE HUMAN MIND IS UNKNOWABLE

Modern neuroscience is keenly aware how great a mystery the human mind is to us. In his book *The Tell-Tale Brain*, neuroscientist Dr. V.S. Ramachandran summarizes this sentiment well:

> How can a three-pound mass of jelly that you can hold in your palm imagine angels, contemplate the meaning of infinity, and even question its own place in the cosmos? Especially awe inspiring is the fact that any single brain, including yours, is made up of atoms that were forged in the hearts of countless, far-flung stars billions of years ago. These particles drifted for eons and light-years until gravity and change brought them together here, now. These atoms now form a conglomerate—your brain—that can not only

ponder the very stars that gave it birth but can also think about its own ability to think and wonder about its own ability to wonder. With the arrival of humans, it has been said, the universe has suddenly become conscious of itself. This, truly, is the greatest mystery of all.[10]

There have been countless studies conducted on psychology and neuroscience, but we have yet to crack the code on how the *mind* works. It is quite fascinating to think how much our very consciousness—so personal to us—is still one of the greatest mysteries of all. There is an unknowability to the mind exceeding almost everything else in the universe.

This mystery living inside each of us might be the closest thing we find to the unknowability of God. It is one while at rest, infinite while at work, eternal in what it knows, and unknowable—just as the divine is the ultimate unknowable mystery. Truly an analogy of the highest form.

PART III

Further Reflections

CHAPTER 9

The Scriptures

"In the beginning, God created the heavens and the earth."

—Genesis 1:1

Fable

"Ready for another adventure?" Sophia asks cheerfully from her place on the ancient seashore.

"Of course," you reply without hesitation. And just like that, you find yourself back in the Old City of Jerusalem. This time you are standing directly in front of the entrance to the Dome of the Rock—the building topped with the large golden dome. The structure is octagonal in shape and covered in exquisite marble work and bright tile mosaics.

"Watch now," Sophia says and passes her hand in front of your view. As your sight returns, something miraculous happens. The exterior wall is now transparent—allowing you to see inside the shrine from your vantage point outside. You are once again speechless as your eyes take in the stunning interior.

You see there are no benches or pews for sitting. Rather, there is a large open area with raw bedrock jutting out through the floor in the center under the dome. Surrounding this open area are pillars supporting the roof. As you look up into the dome, you see it is also tiled in colorful mosaics. There are reds, greens, blues, and blacks creating patterns through a golden background, and graceful Arabic script encircles the dome's edges.

Sophia reminds you that you are looking at the place where Muslims believe the Prophet Muhammad was taken up into Heaven on his horse and given divine visions. She explains that Islamic art does not use human figures to represent the divine. Instead, they utilize geometric patterns and multitudes of color to communicate divine attributes like infinity and eternity.

Beautiful, you think to yourself.

Sophia reminds you that the Dome of the Rock sits atop the very place where the ancient Jewish Temple stood for centuries, making it also the number one holiest site in Judaism and important to Christians as well. "All three monotheistic religions hold this site in high honor. Let's continue on."

The two of you walk down the steps and around the base of the large complex toward one side. As you round the corner, you encounter a stone plaza set in front of a high wall composed of large blocks of white stone. There is a small crowd milling about the plaza.

"Welcome to the Kotel." Sophia gestures toward the structure. "In the West, it is known as the Western Wall."

You look around and observe several people standing near the base of the wall engaged in prayer. Some of them place small pieces of paper into the cracks between the stones while others bow toward the wall in homage. You stand there for a while taking in the sight before you.

"Tell me more about this place," you say.

Sophia begins, "The Western Wall is sacred to Jews because of its proximity to the Foundation Stone lying just behind it, under the Dome of the Rock. If you recall, Judaism considers the Foundation Stone the very place where God created the universe. It is also believed to be the place where He created the first humans, Adam and Eve, and the place where Abraham prepared to sacrifice his son Isaac in obedience to God's command.

"In many ways, this one location marks the beginning of everything. Some refer to it as the Wailing Wall because they see Jews crying out to God in prayer. What many don't realize is they are weeping over the destruction of the Temple of David—the place of God's dwelling and the building representing His original covenant with man. For centuries, people have prayed fervently at the wall, writing down prayer requests and verses of Scripture to place inside the crevices. The place where we're standing is holy ground."

The opening creation narrative of Genesis 1 remains one of my favorite sections of the Bible to this day. I'm not sure why exactly, perhaps because it's beautifully written and steeped in rich symbolism. Maybe because it describes the origins of the universe from the perspective of faith, or possibly because it's the cause of centuries of debate between all types of scholars.

When speaking with friends about the first creation story, I am often surprised at how strong individual beliefs can be about this text. For example, I once made the comment to a friend that the Genesis creation account was a type of ancient poetry and is much more fascinating when interpreted in that context. To this comment came the reply, "I disagree completely; the Bible is God's spoken truth and every word of it is perfectly true just as it's written." I realized later that my friend thought I was diminishing the truth value of the text by implying it is not a word-for-word, detailed account of how the world began. I also realized that honest discussion of this type can be difficult on topics where so much personal belief and identity are involved.

Still, I believe there is a strong argument to be made that story, poetry, and allegory have the power to convey truth in an altogether unique way. In some cases, I think they can convey complex truths much better than straightforward, line-by-line literal accounts can. The first creation story of Genesis, for instance, is a very old text, written by people of a very different culture and time than ours. Just because it's written in another style, however, does not mean its truth is lessened—it only means the truth is packaged in a different communication style than we may be used to.

The Power of Stories

There is good reason why Jesus of Nazareth taught in parables and why Plato wrote in dialogue form. Great teachers throughout history have used the genre of story and allegory to communicate a wide variety of ideas that stick in people's memory. One reason story is such a powerful communication tool is that our minds process and retain information better when it's presented in a plot line. Perhaps this is because our lives play out over time, in a great story of their own. Just think of how easy it is to remember the entire plot of a movie compared to the difficulty of trying to remember the facts in just one chapter of a textbook.

Another reason story has the power to communicate truth in a powerful way is that it allows for a certain variety of interpretation from its listeners. Different people receive individually nuanced lessons from a single story while the main ideas and underlying principles remain the same. This allows for a more personalized learning experience for each listener, creating a larger, individualized impact on all who hear it. It is interesting how you can return to a good story multiple times over and find something new in each reading.

A basic philosophical principle behind the power of story is one we have previously touched on in Plato. An epic tale often follows a universal "form of story," one that fills in the peripheral details according to the author's imagination. Take the famously popular *Star Wars* movies, for example . . . the original three, of course. When George Lucas wrote the storyline for the movies, he relied heavily on a book titled *The Hero with a Thousand Faces*, by Joseph Campbell.

Campbell's research compared hero stories from mythologies around the world and various eras. During his studies, Campbell noticed long-lasting hero mythologies all shared a fundamental, underlying structure—something Plato might call a universal form of hero story. He called this underlying archetype the *hero's journey*, and described it succinctly:

> A hero ventures forth from the world of common day into
> a region of supernatural wonder: fabulous forces are there

encountered and a decisive victory is won: the hero comes back from this mysterious adventure with the power to bestow boons on his fellow man.[1]

Campbell distilled the entire hero mythology down to a very simple template, one that can be universally applied to many different particular stories. Luke Skywalker ventures forth from the common world of Tatooine to encounter the supernatural world of the Jedi. He is trained by Master Yoda and faces his own darkness in the Dagobah swamps. He then arises, empowered with the Force, to save his fellow man. George Lucas masterfully executed a science fiction version of the hero's journey, and so have many others as well.

In *The Lord of the Rings*, Frodo journeys out of his common shire, empowered by the One Ring, to save Middle Earth. In *Spider-Man*, Peter Parker ventures forth from his everyday public-school life, empowered by a genetically engineered spider, to save New York City. In *Harry Potter*, Harry ventures forth from the oppressive world of his relatives, empowered with his magical abilities, to save the whole wizarding world.

These stories, epic in their own right, were planned and written according to a very similar structure—that of the hero's journey archetype. This underlying universal structure is what allows them to communicate deeply moving themes to so many people over multiple generations. While the stories are fiction, they have successfully tapped into a real and lasting truth that resonates within us.

LITERARY STRUCTURE OF GENESIS 1

Good stories reach up into the world of universal forms and bring down a tale clothed in a particular time and culture. To clarify, I don't mean to say that the Genesis creation accounts are stories in the same way that *Star Wars* or *Spider-Man* are stories. Genesis conveys the truth of divine revelation whereas *Star Wars* and *Spider-Man* do not. Still, it is helpful to consider how that divine revelation is communicated. Looking back to the first Genesis creation account, we must ask the following: What is the universal form of story underlying it? What patterns and structure does it use to communicate its truth? Let's look to the text of the first chapter of Genesis as our starting point.

> (1) In the beginning, God created the heavens and the earth. (2) The earth was without form and void, and darkness was upon the face of the deep; and the Spirit of God was moving over the face of the waters.
> (3) And God said, "Let there be light"; and there was light. (4) And God saw that the light was good; and God separated the light from the darkness. (5) God called the light Day, and the darkness he called Night. And there was evening and there was morning, one day.
> (6) And God said, "Let there be a firmament in the midst of the waters, and let it separate the waters from the waters." (7) And God made the firmament and separated the waters which were under the firmament from the waters which were above the firmament. And it was so. (8) And God called the firmament Heaven. And there was evening and there was morning, a second day.
> (9) And God said, "Let the waters under the heavens be gathered together into one place, and let the dry land appear." And it was so. (10) God called the dry land Earth, and the waters that were gathered together he called Seas. And God saw that it was good. (11) And God said, "Let the

earth put forth vegetation, plants yielding seed, and fruit trees bearing fruit in which is their seed, each according to its kind, upon the earth." And it was so. (12) The earth brought forth vegetation, plants yielding seed according to their own kinds, and trees bearing fruit in which is their seed, each according to its kind. And God saw that it was good. (13) And there was evening and there was morning, a third day.

(14) And God said, "Let there be lights in the firmament of the heavens to separate the day from the night; and let them be for signs and for seasons and for days and years, (15) and let them be lights in the firmament of the heavens to give light upon the earth." And it was so. (16) And God made the two great lights, the greater light to rule the day, and the lesser light to rule the night; he made the stars also. (17) And God set them in the firmament of the heavens to give light upon the earth, (18) to rule over the day and over the night, and to separate the light from the darkness. And God saw that it was good. (19) And there was evening and there was morning, a fourth day.

(20) And God said, "Let the waters bring forth swarms of living creatures, and let birds fly above the earth across the firmament of the heavens." (21) So God created the great sea monsters and every living creature that moves, with which the waters swarm, according to their kinds, and every winged bird according to its kind. And God saw that it was good. (22) And God blessed them saying, "Be fruitful and multiply and fill the waters in the seas, and let birds multiply on the earth." (23) And there was evening and there was morning, a fifth day.

(24) And God said, "Let the earth bring forth living

creatures according to their kinds: cattle and creeping things and beasts of the earth according to their kinds." And it was so. (25) And God made the beasts of the earth according to their kinds and the cattle according to their kinds, and everything that creeps upon the ground according to its kind. And God saw that it was good. (26) Then God said, "Let us make man in our image, after our likeness; and let them have dominion over the fish of the sea, and over the birds of the air, and over the cattle, and over all of the earth, and over every creeping thing that creeps upon the earth."

(27) So God created man in his own image, in the image of God he created him; male and female he created them. (28) And God blessed them, and God said to them, "Be fruitful and multiply, and fill the earth and subdue it; and have dominion over the fish of the sea and over the birds of the air and over every living thing that moves upon the earth." (29) And God said, "Behold, I have given you every plant yielding seed which is upon the face of all the earth, and every tree with seeds in its fruit; you shall have them for food. (30) And to every beast of the earth, and to every bird of the air, and to everything that creeps on the earth, everything that has the breath of life, I have given every green plant for food." And it was so. (31) And God saw everything that he had made, and behold, it was very good. And there was evening and there was morning, a sixth day.[2]

It is important to note that the first creation account in Genesis did not start out as a written text at all. The story was passed down through generation after generation by the spoken word long before it was ever written down anywhere. It was told from parents to children around campfires and discussed among ancient scholars in primitive classrooms. The Genesis 1 account was cultural and religious tradition, passed on from believer to believer throughout hundreds and thousands of years. And then, at some later time, it was written down and preserved.

In their book *The Old Testament Survey, Second Edition*, William LaSor, David Hubbard, and Frederic Bush write, "The inspired authors of the primeval prologue (Gen. 1: 1–11) drew on the manner of speaking about origins that was part of their culture and literary traditions. Ch. 1 needs to be read in light of creation accounts from Mesopotamia."[3] The ancient world from which Genesis 1 arose spoke in story form to communicate their complex beliefs about subjects like the creation of the world. The structure behind the Genesis creation account is marked by a distinct literary genre common to the ancient Near East; however, it is no longer a common way of writing today.

To be sure, there was careful logic used in building the sentence structure of the creation account. *The Old Testament Survey* identifies this structure as having seven parts.

1. An introductory word of announcement, "God said . . ."

2. A creative word of command, "Let there be . . ."

3. A summary word of accomplishment, "And it was so . . ."

4. A descriptive word of accomplishment, "God made . . . ," "The earth brought forth . . ."

5. A descriptive word of naming or blessing, "God called . . . ," "God blessed . . ."

6. An evaluative word of naming or blessing, "God saw that it was good . . ."

7. A concluding word of temporal framework, "It was evening and it was morning, day . . ."

At its heart, this is a form of ancient poetry. Anyone familiar with composing haikus in grade school can see the similarities in the previous sentence structure. It follows a very distinct formula and uses deep symbology to communicate really big ideas. To acknowledge this fact does not make what it's communicating any less true. Rather, identifying the underlying structure helps lead the reader to a fuller understanding of the story. To argue that the first creation account of Genesis should be read as a literal accounting of the creation of the world is to completely miss what its author is trying to say. If we start off by getting the underlying structure wrong, we risk missing out on the deeper meaning altogether.

Let's look at some of the specific things we can learn from Genesis given this poetic framework. First, the universe and everything in it had *a beginning*. There was a Creator and this Creator was the First Cause of everything that now exists. Second, the Creator created with *intentional order*. God made the earth according to a blueprint, bringing order out of chaos. Third, humanity is the *crown of creation*. The earth and all its wonderful, living diversity are gifts for us to steward. The Creator placed His unique image into humanity alone. We are the ones set apart in a special way from the other animals and are responsible for taking care of God's gift of creation.

Is Genesis 1 poetry? Yes. And the truth it conveys is not lessened because of the literary genre. Was the world created in seven twenty-four-hour periods? Maybe not—but that doesn't automatically make the poetry of Genesis false. The truth it conveys remains clear when read in the proper context. The world had a beginning, was made by a Creator, with a specific order and hierarchy in mind.

Word Choice

To unlock the deeper meaning in the Scriptures, it can be helpful to look at the specific words the author chose when writing. Sometimes overlooked, certain words have the power to reshape the way we interpret the story. Let's look at a few of the ancient words in the first two lines of Genesis 1:

"In the beginning . . ." Here, the Hebrew word used is *reshith*, which translates simply as "a beginning." As we've discussed previously, this simple start to the Bible carries massive weight. There was a beginning for the created universe and a beginning for life. As we touched upon in earlier chapters, scholars—including Plato, Aristotle, and Einstein—believed space was an eternal, static reality. They thought it had always been here, without a beginning, existing in a continuous steady state. Centuries ago, the Genesis author used this one simple word, *reshith*, to reveal what science has only recently discovered.

"In the beginning, God created the heavens and the earth." The word used for *created* is the Hebrew verb *bara*. The word for *heavens* is *shamayim*, which translates to "heaven" or "sky," and would have included the stars, the cosmos, and all heavenly bodies within them. The Hebrew word for *earth* is *erets*, which translates to "earth" or "ground," but includes all the known lands. There is a larger, synergistic meaning here because the words for *heaven* and *earth* are used together. When combined, *shamayim* and *erets* would have meant everything contained in the material world of ancient experience, including all matter, land, sea, sky, heavens, cosmos, stars, and planets. In this light, the text could be read as, "In the beginning, God created everything."

Next, we move to the second line of Genesis, where the text begins to describe this new creation. "The earth was *without form and void* . . ." The Hebrew words for *without form* and *void* are the phrase *tohu wa-bohu*. *Tohu* translates to something along the lines of "confusion" or "formlessness." *Bohu* means something like "emptiness." When combined, they communicate the idea that the original creation was something difficult to describe and even more difficult to understand. Some scholars interpret this phrase to mean God brought order out of chaos or understanding out of mystery. In any case, the original, creative work of God could be described as having no human comprehension, no form for our minds to grasp.

The point here is that looking at the original language can help us understand the variety of interpretive possibilities sometimes lost when reading solely in translation. If we pause briefly and consider the slippery nature of modern English, we can see that words often carry multiple meanings depending on context and emphasis. It should not surprise us then that the creation story in Genesis has been interpreted in varying ways. No single interpretation warrants a destruction of belief, however, because God's unknowability assumes a mystery never fully reachable and varying interpretations of Genesis can still fit within the broader framework of faith.

The Influence of Greece

By now, the Greek influence on biblical translation should be jumping off the page. Recall from earlier chapters that the city of Alexandria, Egypt, became the center for Greek culture and the storehouse of collective human knowledge at that time. It was there in Alexandria that the Hebrew Torah was likely first translated into Greek. This Greek translation became the accepted version of the Old Testament that Matthew, Mark, Luke, and John relied upon to write the Gospels.

The ancient translation of Hebrew into Greek is referred to as the *Septuagint*, meaning "the Translation of the Seventy." Legend has it that seventy-two renowned scholars, six from each of the twelve tribes of Israel, were invited by the pharaoh of Egypt to translate the Hebrew Torah individually. When they came back with their translations, all seventy-two versions miraculously matched in every way. Obviously, this legend was told as a validation for the accuracy of the text and may or may not be factual. After its completion, however, the Septuagint translation of the Hebrew Scriptures gained massive adoption, owing mostly to the dying use of ancient Hebrew within society and the growing use of the Greek language.

This history is important because modern Christians may not realize how strongly the Greek language, culture, and context have colored our understanding of the Bible. Not only was the whole New Testament written in Greek, but the New Testament authors also relied on Greek translations of the Old Testament as their source texts for understanding it. A Greek lens has colored the Christian understanding of the Bible in almost every aspect. In his book *Translation of the Seventy*, Scripture scholar Edmon Gallagher emphasizes this influence of the Greek language on Scripture:

> The New Testament was written in Greek. By my count, it quotes the Old Testament 344 times, always in Greek. The one partial exception is the Cry of Dereliction at the

Crucifixion, "Eloi, Eloi. Lama sabachthani" (Mark 15:34; cf. Matt. 27:46), a quotation of Psalm 22:1 in Aramaic. But the Gospels neither mark these words as a quotation (i.e., they do not introduce it with something like "Jesus said, it is written . . .") nor leave them in Aramaic only, since they immediately provide a Greek translation. Every other quotation of the Old Testament is in Greek; what Greek version of the scriptures were the New Testament writers quoting? The easy answer is that they were quoting the Septuagint.[4]

Theologian Joseph Ratzinger, who later became Pope Benedict XVI, took the relationship between Scripture and the Greek intellectual tradition a step further. He believed God intentionally raised up the philosophical tradition of Greece at the appointed time when the New Testament Scriptures would first emerge. In his *Introduction to Christianity*, he writes, "I am convinced that at bottom it was no mere accident that the Christian message, in the period when it was taking shape, first entered the Greek world and there merged with the inquiry into understanding, into truth."[5]

The Roman Catholic and Greek Orthodox Churches both chose the Greek Septuagint translations of the Old Testament for their official canons of Scripture. After the Protestant Reformation in the sixteenth century, however, most Protestant denominations rejected the Septuagint and returned to a more direct Hebrew translation of the texts.

If you are a modern reader of the Bible, you have likely become accustomed to Greek interpretations of certain passages of the Old Testament—one of which we find in the second verse of Genesis 1. Here again, we return to the great conversation begun by Plato, Aristotle, and Greek philosophy. The same conversation that influenced most of monotheistic theology has also found its way into the interpretations of our most sacred texts. Let's take a closer look at this Greek influence.

"The earth was *without form* and *void* . . ." What does it mean in Greek philosophy to be without form? In Plato and Aristotle's worldviews, it's a big deal. How might they have explained the original Genesis creation having no form at all? Interestingly, both philosophers offered their thoughts on the hypothetical condition of matter having no form. They were doing the work of philosophy, thinking about matter separated out from form. They did not have Genesis 1 in mind necessarily, but their conclusions applied to the creation story are fascinating and demonstrate our continued assertion that the wonder of reason supports faith; it is not antagonistic to it.

In *Timaeus*, Plato provides a new category of being that's distinct from his worlds of material objects and universal forms. He calls this state of being "a receptacle of all coming to be." He is referring to a theoretical state of matter completely separated from form altogether. Plato writes of this unique state:

> It both continually receives all things, and has never taken on a form similar to any of the things that enter it in any way. For it is laid down by nature as a recipient of impressions for everything, being changed and formed variously by the things that enter it, and because of them it appears different at different times.[6]

Plato's "receptacle of all coming to be" is a type of matter that has the potential to receive all forms into itself. It is pure potential. This matter has not committed to any particular form but is a recipient for them all.

Aristotle, as was his custom, criticized his teacher and then built upon his ideas. For Aristotle, the forms simply cannot exist on their own apart from matter. He sought to explain the hypothetical idea of matter apart from form in a different way, using what he called *prime matter*.

Aristotle introduced prime matter as the most basic substance underlying the elements that make up material things. The basic elements were earth, air, fire, and water, and the Greeks believed each element had the power to change back and forth into the other elements under the right conditions. Prime matter, then, was the fundamental substance underlying everything in the material world.

Aristotle, like Plato, also described prime matter as pure potentiality. It is matter with no form, having the power to take on any form. It can become anything and all things. It is on the opposite end of the spectrum as the Unmoved Mover. One is pure potential to become and the other is infinite actuality with no potential to become anything more.

Plato and Aristotle's descriptions of matter separated from form prove useful in combining the revelation of Scripture with the discoveries of modern science. In many ways, the primordial energy soup of the Big Bang was matter without form. It was all potential-to-be, ready to take on new forms: stars, planets, life, and humanity. As Plato said, "It is laid down by nature as a recipient of impressions for everything, being changed and formed variously by the things that enter it."[7] God created the earth *tohu wa-bohu*, *without form* and *void*.

Separating Out

Genesis 1:1 says, "In the beginning God created the heavens and the earth." At the start, we see a single creative act of God, denoted by the word *bara*. After the first creative act, however, the author switches to a different action verb to continue the story. After God creates the heavens and the earth, He begins a series of differentiations where He separates out new things from the original creation. This distinction is important because God is not creating new things out of nothing as he did in His first act. Rather he is adding in forms to the prime matter and bringing new things out of it. Here begins a divine symphony of separation, developing a growing complexity of created things. God gives to the formless matter of His original creation a multitude of new forms.

Genesis 1:3–5 says, "(3) And God said, 'Let there be light'; and there was light. (4) And God saw that the light was good; and God separated the light from the darkness. (5) God called the light Day, and the darkness he called Night. And there was evening and there was morning, one day." In this section that immediately follows the creation of the heavens and the earth, God speaks and divides out. Notice, the verse does not say God created light; rather He says, "Let there be light," and separates it out from the darkness. He pulls light out from the initial creation already present.

The Hebrew word for *God said* is *amar*. *Amar* translates as "to utter" or "to say," which is how it appears most commonly in the first creation account in Genesis. *Amar* is also used in other parts of Scripture to mean things like "to command," "to designate," or "to inform." The words used for *separate* are versions of the Hebrew word *badal*, which translates specifically as "to separate" or "divide out." This pattern is then repeated throughout the text as God commands the land to appear from out of the waters and the earth to put forth all kinds of vegetation. Again, from one creation, He divides out a growing complexity of diversification.

This is where the ancient Near East poetic structure of Genesis has a strong influence on the text. God repeats a set pattern of speaking, separating out new things from the original creation, calling them by a new name and declaring them good. Each repeating pattern is depicted as its own day of creation. The author used the idea of days to imply a set period of time and order, relying on the common experience of a day as an effective form of communication.

The Genesis creation account seen through the light of Greek philosophy's prime matter provides a fascinating depth of interpretation. God creates everything at once; it is matter in a state of pure potential to become anything and everything. It is the simplest of things holding within itself the power to become an endless complexity of diverse, new things. God creates *bara*. He then speaks forms into the formless and void. As He adds in the first basic forms, matter responds by taking shape. Light differentiates from darkness; the waters separate out, and the land is infused with vegetation and animals of all kinds. Then, humanity is given the image of God in the form of a new rational capacity. Creation culminates in those able to see the unseen world of forms infused into the prime matter of creation.

THE SECOND CREATION ACCOUNT

Let's now turn our attention to the story of the Garden of Eden in the second creation account of Genesis 2. Here we will consider an example of what interpreting the Scriptures in light of scientific discovery might look like. First, let's look at the text:

In the day that the Lord God made the earth and the heavens, (5) when no plant of the field was yet in the earth and no herb of the field had yet sprung up—for the Lord God had not caused it to rain upon the earth, and there was no man to till the ground; (6) but a mist went up from the earth and watered the whole face of the ground—(7) then the Lord God formed man of dust from the ground, and breathed into his nostrils the breath of life; and man became a living being. (8) And the Lord God planted a garden in Eden, in the east; and there he put the man whom he had formed. (9) And out of the ground the Lord God made to grow every tree that is pleasant to the sight and good for food, the tree of life also in the midst of the garden, and the tree of the knowledge of good and evil.

(10) A river flowed out of Eden to water the garden, and there it divided and became four rivers. (11) The name of the first is Pishon; it is the one which flows around the whole land of Havilah, where there is gold; (12) and the gold of that land is good; bdellium and onyx stone are there. (13) The name of the second river is Gihon; it is the one which flows around the whole land of Cush. (14) And the name of the third river is Tigris, which flows east of Assyria. And the fourth river is the Euphrates.

(15) The Lord God took the man and put him in the garden of Eden to till it and keep it. (16) And the Lord God commanded the man, saying, "You may freely eat of every tree of the garden; (17) but of the tree of the knowledge of good and evil you shall not eat, for in the day that you eat of it you shall die."

(18) Then the Lord God said, "It is not good that the

man should be alone; I will make him a helper fit for him." (19) So out of the ground the Lord God formed every beast of the field and every bird of the air, and brought them to the man to see what he would call them; and whatever the man called every living creature, that was its name. (20) The man gave names to all cattle, and to the birds of the air, and to every beast of the field; but for the man there was not found a helper fit for him. (21) So the Lord God caused a deep sleep to fall upon the man, and while he slept took one of his ribs and closed up its place with flesh; (22) and the rib which the Lord God had taken from the man he made into a woman and brought her to the man. (23) Then the man said,

"This at last is bone of my bones
and flesh of my flesh;
she shall be called Woman,
because she was taken out of Man."

(24) Therefore a man leaves his father and his mother and cleaves to his wife, and they become one flesh. (25) And the man and his wife were both naked and were not ashamed.[8]

While the first Genesis account provides a systematic telling of the order of creation in poetic form, the second account relies on narrative form to highlight the central role of humanity's relationship with God and the world. The order of creation appears different compared to the first account, but that's because the story is conveying a different message altogether. As we've said before, reading either creation account like a textbook means we risk missing the deeper meaning within.

Considering modern scientific findings, the question arises, can this story still be true? I believe the answer to that question is yes. The historical events might have played out differently than in the Genesis story, but the deeper meaning of the narrative remains the same. Personally, I've always wondered what the story would've looked like from a historical perspective. Join me in a little thought experiment as we imagine what the story of the Garden of Eden could have looked like. A word of warning, however—this exercise may cause some cognitive dissonance!

A RETELLING OF THE GARDEN

The time is around three hundred thousand years in the past. The setting is the verdant grasslands of Africa—lush and green—a climate much different than today's. There is a tribe of hominins living in the lowlands, hunting prey and gathering fruits and herbs for food. This particular group is much like the multitude of other groups roaming Africa and nearby parts of the world. They have been evolving on this path for six million years, since separating out from the ancestral line that would become modern chimpanzees. It is a regular group of hominins, nothing particularly special about them.

On an ordinary day like so many others, a baby is born. It is a male, normal in appearance. This baby, however, is unique beyond measure. It is the first primate endowed by God with an immortal, human soul.

The baby grows up alongside his parents as a member of the

tribe just like the rest of the children. At the age of seven or eight, however, the boy begins to show exceptional mental ability. He notices that he is different from his parents and different from the other hominins of his tribe and wonders why. He attempts to communicate with others in his group on a deeper level, but his attempts consistently fall on deaf ears. They treat him like one of the family but have no interest in anything more than finding food, shelter, and rest.

As he grows into a young man, he begins building structures with his hands and uses them for various functions—shelters to keep off the rain and tools for cutting. The young man notices there is beauty in the world around him and desires to communicate this, to celebrate it. He draws pictures of animals in the dirt and paints landscapes in bright colors on stone walls.

More than anything, the young man is aware of a powerful Presence alive in the world. Though invisible to his sight, the Presence remains always with him, always close by. The young man feels drawn to spend time alone in the company of the Presence and he leaves for extended periods of time away from the others. The Presence fills him with an overwhelming sense of joy. Life is good and there is a garden of peace within his soul.

Around the age of fifteen, the young man, now fully self-sufficient, lives off by himself in a hut he built with his hands. One day, a neighboring tribe of hominins passes through the vicinity of his dwelling. The hut is interesting to them, so they stop to inspect. The young man shows gestures of hospitality, allowing the small group to satisfy their curiosity, knowing they will look around and move on.

This kind of thing happens from time to time, but today something is different. Today there is a female with the new tribe walking by herself near the back of the group. The young woman is not inspecting the hut like the others; instead, she is staring intently at the young man.

The young man senses the Presence move within him, so he approaches the woman, studying her eyes as he goes. He senses that the same Presence is also living within her. She smiles at the young man and in that moment, he realizes for the first time that he is no longer alone. There is another, just like him, alive in the world. The man sees the woman for what she is and the woman, in turn, sees the man. In their hearts, they say to the Presence, "This one at last is my equal."

This attempt at a retelling of the Garden of Eden is my way of reconciling the world of faith with what we are discovering from the world of science. I'm aware it likely won't sit well with some, but I wrote it as an example of how the beloved story from Genesis remains true in light of modern scientific findings.

In this story, God still forms man from the *dust of the ground*; it just takes a bit longer than the Genesis story portrays. If the earth formed 4.5 billion years ago, and life came from the elements within the earth, then the first humans came from those elements as well. The main idea remains, but the details are slightly different.

God breathes life into man by placing an immortal soul within him at his conception. The man is a *living being* in a way the animals are not. The man is alive, in a higher sense, because he now has the powers of a rational soul and the ability to know God.

Recall Michelangelo's *The Creation of Adam*, where God is

riding on a mind-shaped cloud bringing Adam the gift of rationality. If you look closely, God has a second gift in store for him as well. In the painting, God is depicted with His arm around the woman, Eve, as she rides with God on the cloud. God gives to humanity the dual gift of rationality and intimate, human love. Where before Adam was alone in a world that did not understand him, he and Eve are now seen, known, and loved by one another. Their love will go on to bear fruit in children and create the first rational family. In this way, God deepens His image in humanity further. The family who sees, knows, and loves one another becomes a living icon of the Christian Trinitarian God.

In my story, Eve is not formed directly from the rib of Adam; instead, she is made in the same way that Adam was—her body through evolutionary processes over millions of years and her soul given as a gift from God at the appointed time. Together, however, they fulfill the meaning of "bone of my bones and flesh of my flesh," a phrase used multiple times in the Hebrew Bible to mean the strongest bond of loyalty in family and friendship.

Does this story fit perfectly with the one in Genesis 2? No, it doesn't. But I believe the Genesis narrative provides us with the deeper truth of the matter, that of God's special relationship with humanity and of humanity's unique role in creation. Scripture reveals the deeper meaning while science uncovers the details of how the story played out in time.

THE QUR'AN

The faith of Islam holds the Jewish book of Genesis and the prophet Moses in great respect. Judaism, Islam, and Christianity are all descended from the Abrahamic line and are therefore known as the Abrahamic religions. Islamic belief, however, holds that the Jewish Torah and the words of Moses have come down to us corrupted and changed. They are no longer reliable texts in the original condition that God gave them. Islam respects the legacy of the Scriptures and the words of the prophets that came before, but only the book of the Qur'an and the words of the Prophet Muhammad are the clear truth as Allah intended it. For Islam, the Qur'an and the Prophet Muhammad are the final and complete revelation of God to the world.

While the Qur'an does not have an opening creation account like Genesis, it does have a good deal to say about the origins of the world in various passages. Astonishingly, we find very similar descriptions of creation as we find in Genesis and in Greece.

Verse 21:30, for example, says, "Do the disbelievers not realize the heavens and the earth were once one mass, then We split them apart?" Here we find a strikingly similar passage to the formless and void creation of Genesis. The heavens and the earth were combined as "one mass," inferring that God created everything in existence all at once. The Qur'an provides the same image of creation starting out as a perfect unity. The very next act of Allah in this Qur'anic creation verse is to separate and divide out, or "split them apart." God is creating and then separating out—just as in Genesis—just as in science.

In a separate passage of the Qur'an, Allah is described as creating the world in a six-day period, similar to Genesis's six days of creation. Qur'an verse 7:54 says, "Indeed your Lord is Allah Who created the heavens and the earth in six days." The Arabic word used here for *day* is *youm*. Muslim scholars point out that this same word, *youm*, is used differently in other places in the

Qur'anic text. In each separate instance, it denotes a different measurement of time. In passage 22:47, for example, *youm* is used to mean one thousand years. In verse 70:4, one *youm* refers to fifty thousand years. The Qur'an is not opposed to the use of symbolic measurements of time to communicate an ordered period, just as we have seen from the ancient Mesopotamian poetry of Genesis.

Interestingly, the next line from verse 21:30 is a passage that reads, "And We created from water every living thing." Could this passage be referring to the original single-celled bacteria of the ancient seas? The God of Genesis separates land out of the water and then life arises up out of the land. There is an intermediary step, but first there is water and then there is life. Similarly, in the Qur'an, Allah "created from water every living thing." During Aristotle's time of reflection on the island of Lesbos, he too deduced that life must have first arisen from the water. In our modern day, science holds that life evolved out of the seas and onto the land. Perhaps there is more in common here than we first thought.

CHAPTER 10

The Wonder of It All

"One cannot help but be in awe when he contemplates the mysteries of eternity, of life, of the marvelous structure of reality."

—Albert Einstein

Fable

You are sitting on the back porch enjoying the coolness of a fall evening. You rock leisurely in your favorite chair as the sun sets slowly in the distant sky, painting orange and pink strokes across a canvas of white clouds. You are quite old now; so many years have passed that it's getting hard to remember exactly just how old you are.

That's okay, you muse to yourself. *All in all, it's been a good life.* As you reflect on decades of memories, your mind rests on the good times throughout the years. You think of the joyful moments with family and friends, as well as the times of growth and discovery. *Don't forget all the years of struggle and hardship*, you remind yourself. But most of those difficult times are behind you now—only the aches and pains of an aging body remain. *A regular human life*, you think. *Not so special in the bigger picture, but still . . . a good life.* This makes you smile.

It's been many years since you last saw Sophia; still, she continues to hold a special place in your heart. The wisdom she brought to your life is deep within you now. During the quieter moments alone, such as an evening like this, her words resurface, bringing on fresh waves of wonder. When this happens, the world becomes alive again, as if you've discovered the insights all over for the first time. Her wisdom has added a depth to your life that you're truly grateful for.

You have been growing more tired lately. You come to your rocking chair every morning and every evening, as often as possible really, to gaze out at the hills in the west. Sometimes you focus on a good memory, and other times you mull over one of your adventures with Sophia. Mostly, though, you just sit in your favorite chair and breathe in the beauty before you. This evening, the sunset has a special character to it; perhaps it's a bit more vibrant than usual. You rock slowly back and forth as the sun completes its descent behind the hills. Then, you close your eyes for a little rest, feeling the warmth of the sun's final rays on your face.

"Hello, old friend."

The greeting startles you awake. Your eyes attempt to open but are blinded by an intensity of light beyond anything you've ever experienced. It's as if the sun came to rest in your backyard instead of setting behind the hills. Despite your best efforts, all you can make out is the figure of a woman standing in the sea of light.

"Sophia?" you ask.

"Yes, it's me."

Out of pure excitement, you stand up and walk to the edge of the porch, shielding your eyes as you go.

"Sophia, what's happening?"

"Don't be afraid; come with me. I have one more place to show you. I promise this will be the best one of all."

As you walk down the porch steps and into the yard, you no longer feel the pains in your body. Your joints are working well now, as if you're young again. For a moment, you glance back at your chair on the porch. You are stunned to see yourself still sitting there. Your eyes closed, head resting on the chair back as if sleeping peacefully. You don't know what to think.

"Don't turn back," Sophia says. "Keep walking this way."

Her voice hits your ears with its usual steady assurance. You keep walking toward the woman clothed with the sun. By the time you reach her, your eyes have adjusted to the light. You can see that she is smiling, with arms open to embrace you.

"It is so good to see you again; are you ready for one last adventure?"

"Yes," you say, then ask hesitantly, "I guess this is the end for me?"

Sophia is visibly taken aback by the question—as if unable to process what you're asking.

"No, my friend, not the end at all! Quite the opposite, in fact—I am taking you to my home," she continues, her eyes now glowing like the light all around her.

"Where I come from there are no 'ends,' there is only new discovery. It is a place where beauty and knowledge are ever ancient and ever new. I promise you will not be disappointed." She ends on a triumphal note, clearly proud of her homeland.

"That does sound like quite the adventure," you respond as the memory of your first encounter with Sophia at the office building returns to mind. Without needing to consider it this time, you say, "I'm ready."

You take Sophia's hand and walk with her into the intensity

of burning light. The light is fierce but there is no pain. Instead, a peace beyond understanding fills you entirely—a peace so deep it turns to overflowing joy and sweetness. The brightness of the light does not fade, though now your eyes can see clearly. What you see in the light lies far beyond description. One word, however, rises to mind.

Wonder.

The Problem Revisited

In chapter 1, we discussed the difficult task of holding faith and science united in our minds. It is a tension that occurs within ourselves, oftentimes without us even realizing that it's happening. We use one mindset to research the marvels of science and a completely different one in search of the wonder of God. Worse than that, many of us end up believing faith and science are incompatible altogether and feel forced to choose between one or the other.

What ancient wisdom shows us, however, is quite the opposite from this dichotomy. Philosophers like Plato and Aristotle approached the divine from a scientific mindset. Using observation, logic, complex reasoning, and debate, they arrived at the need for a necessary existence to explain the world around them.

Then, theologians saw the value in Greek wisdom and took up the baton of reason in the pursuit of the things of faith. Philo and Maimonides from Judaism, Avicenna and Averroes from Islam, and Augustine and Aquinas from Christianity—each answered the call to synthesize Greek principles with their respective faiths. From these syntheses, we arrived at a rational image of God accepted within all three of the major monotheistic religions: Judaism, Islam, and Christianity. A God who conforms to the basic tenets of human reason but is not defined by that reason. A God who can unite the mystery of faith with the logic of science.

God is nonphysical, one, infinite, eternal, and unknowable. A God explained through negative terms by what He is not and in analogical terms by what He is like. These attributes provide us with a glimpse into the divine while also maintaining respect for the great, ultimately unknowable mystery that is God.

THE REVELATION OF SCIENCE

It is fascinating to think that the greatest scientific wonders occurred in total obscurity, without anyone present other than God to witness them. Like the humble birth of Christ, the most spectacular miracles of science happened under the most ordinary of everyday circumstances.

The Big Bang expanded an entire universe out of absolute nothingness some 13.8 billion years ago. The atmospheric conditions were quietly prepared, over billions of years, until the world was ready for the miracle of life. The human soul and the power of the rational mind arrived on the scene after millennia of evolution readied the primate line for the gift of all gifts. No fanfare, no celebrations, no recognition that these things even happened—until millions of years after the fact. In silence and obscurity, the greatest of miracles occurred, and we are the fortunate ones who get to receive them today and speculate on how it all happened. Simply amazing.

The Universe

The universe was one and indivisible at its very beginning. It displayed a clear similarity to the oneness of God. Matter = Energy and $F_g = F_s = F_w = F_{em}$ just as in God, His essence = What He is = What He is doing = What He knows = His existence. The early universe was Plato's and Aristotle's prime matter, void of all form. It contained within it the potential to become what it is today and even more as it continues to move into the future.

Every planet and every star in the observable universe was present as radiation energy at the Big Bang. All one hundred billion stars in our Milky Way galaxy, as well as the trillions upon trillions of other stars from the two trillion galaxies within the known universe—all were present. Beyond that even, every star and every planet from the unobservable universe, places we will never see due to the inability of their light to reach us, were also present in this same moment. The oneness of the universe at its beginning is impossible to comprehend but fascinating nonetheless.

As the void of space races out in every direction, we see a real attempt of the physical world to imitate God in His infinity. The essence of God is nonfinite, having no boundaries and encompassing everything within Himself. For 13.8 billion years, space has been expanding and accelerating outward, reaching unfathomable size by now, showing no signs of stopping anytime soon. Yet, God is bigger than even this.

As you gaze out into the night sky at distant stars millions of light-years away, it is comforting to think that what exists out there is just like what exists right here. The uniformity of the universe represents the simple uniformity of God's essence. He is the same thing at every moment and in every place. God is already way out there in deep space in the exact same way He is present to this particular place and this particular time.

Life

It is a real possibility that Earth might contain the only intelligent life in the universe. Perhaps there is water with living microbes out there, but to date we have yet to find any concrete signs of higher intelligence from our search of faraway exoplanets. No radio communications coming from deep space, no aberrant light sources signaling advanced alien civilizations. No life out there yet, only evidence of water and ice.

Life is a tremendous gift we must cherish and protect. This was the first command given by God to Adam and Eve in Genesis 1:28:

> And God blessed them and God said to them, "Be fruitful and multiply, and fill the earth and subdue it; and have dominion over the fish of the sea and over the birds of the air and over every living thing that moves upon the earth."[1]

Like the larger universe, life bears the image of God in its own analogical form. It began as one, in single-celled bacteria, and now moves slowly through time toward infinite diversity. Simple cells bearing within them the potential to become every living thing started the journey that's taken billions of years so far. And it's still going, evolving into ever more complex diversity; life pushes on through periods of intense hardship, environmental stress, and mass extinctions. As Dr. Ian Malcolm says in the classic movie *Jurassic Park*, "Life finds a way."

The origin of life remains hidden from our science. We understand its complexities and we marvel at its beauty, but we have yet to crack the code on how to create it from nonliving material. The magic of life remains a mystery. In that way, it also reveals something of God's image.

The Human Mind

Homo sapiens stand apart from the other animals in a very unique way. On one hand, we are a part of the long lineage of life's evolutionary processes. We are an animal, like all the others, and we bear this truth deep in our DNA. According to the second creation account of Genesis 2, "The Lord God formed man of dust from the ground and breathed into his nostrils the breath of life; and man became a living being."[2] We come from the dust of the earth, from the matter of this physical world—the same matter present at the first moment of the Big Bang. But, on the other hand, there is something more within us, something unique that raises us higher than the other animals.

Genesis 1:26 says, "Then God said, 'Let us make man in our image, after our likeness . . .'" Humanity bears the image of God in a very special way, most notably in our rational capacity to know the unseen world. The content we have journeyed through in this book is evidence that we can see and know these higher things. We can use our reason to discover God, discover the universe, discover the beauty of life, and even to know our very selves. It is this capacity to know timeless things that tells us there is also something timeless within us.

The mind at rest reveals the oneness of God in a way similar to the Big Bang and the first cells of life. It is the *tabula rasa*, the blank slate, with the potential to know all things. The near-infinite variety of thoughts and complex ideas we contemplate as humans displays our resemblance to the infinity of God. Even ideas themselves have a timelessness that lives on throughout the generations, passing from one mind to the next.

We are at the same time mortal and immortal. We've been given a gift beyond anything in the universe. We are the only ones who can receive the universe for what it is. We were made in God's image and after His likeness.

ALL THINGS COME FROM GOD AND MOVE TOWARD GOD

Each of the great miracles of science bears the analogy of God's image. All three begin in a state of oneness and indivisibility. There is an undeniable unity in the initial radiation state of the early universe, in the necessary structure of the first cells of life, and in the blank slate of the human mind at rest.

All three analogies then move to fulfill a potential for infinity. The current size of the universe and the mind-blowing number of galaxies out there beyond our observable sphere. The immense diversity of life on Earth with each life-form continually evolving into whatever direction the environment shapes it next. And the near-infinite number of potential ideas the human mind is capable of thinking. All of these show forth as analogies of the infinite, unbounded God.

The three analogies of science play out over a painstakingly long time—13.8 billion years since the start of it all and four billion years since the evolution of life first began its journey on this planet. The time scales are too big for us to truly comprehend. In this way, they speak to us of God's eternity and His existence outside of time. The human mind, capable of participating in the great conversation of philosophy, has the ability to know the timeless world of ideas. The mind, too, reveals God's timelessness and eternity in its own unique way.

Finally, each mystery of science bears within it the ultimate unknowability of God. Our physics breaks down when confronted with the Big Bang singularity. Our laboratories fail when attempting to re-create life from its constituent parts. The beginning of time and the origin of life remain elusive to our knowledge. In an even more profound way, our minds remain one of the greatest mysteries in the universe yet to be solved. We know a lot about psychology, brain biology, and neuroscience, yet we cannot *solve* the wonder of the human mind. It remains a mystery hidden from our knowledge just as God's essence remains similarly hidden.

THE THREE MONOTHEISTIC FAITHS

While I did not write this book as a defense of the Christian faith, I would like to take a moment to offer two reasons why I believe Christianity contains the fullness of truth, as I feel they are pertinent to our discussion here. The first thing I appreciate about the Christian faith is the way in which it completes and fulfills Judaism instead of trying to cancel it out. There is a beautiful development of theology that begins in the revelation of YHWH to His chosen people and finds fulfillment in the coming of Christ as the foretold Messiah. I love that Christianity retains and respects so much of its Jewish roots in this manner.

The second thing I find fascinating about Christianity is the way in which Jesus performs miracles. He heals a blind man by rubbing mud on his eyes, He calls His followers to be baptized with water, He turns bread into His body and wine into His blood, and in His greatest act, He offers up His life so that we might gain access to everlasting life.

Jesus uses the everyday stuff of earth (mud, water, bread, wine, etc.) to communicate the divine. Most often we find in the Gospels that there is no fanfare and there are no fireworks when

Jesus acts. His miracles are at the same time natural and supernatural. Even in His very person, Jesus is both natural (fully man) and supernatural (fully God). I can't help but notice the similarities between the miracles of Jesus and the miracles of science we've discussed here at length. If Jesus really is the second person of the Trinity and the Word (Logos) of God, then it makes sense that the miracles He performed while creating the world should be of a similar type and quality to the miracles He performed while incarnate in the world. Indeed, that seems to be exactly what we find. In that way, the continuity of Christianity with Judaism extends back even further to include the beginning of space and time as well.

Returning now to monotheism in general, recall our discussion on the foundation of reason underlying the three major monotheistic faiths. Judaism, Islam, and Christianity each believe in a single God who bears the attributes of being nonphysical, one, infinite, eternal, and unknowable. It is a search into what YHWH, Allah, and the Trinity must be like—and what each of these concepts of God have in common.

Most of the synthesizer theologians throughout history have agreed that the Scriptures are best interpreted in the light of reason. If we are not careful, our tendency to over-anthropomorphize God as the old man on a throne of clouds who acts in human ways and feels human emotions can end up making Him smaller in our minds. We can come to forget the great mystery.

The Judeo-Christian Scriptures are a collection of documents whose origins span thousands of years. They were written by a variety of authors in many different contexts and cultures. The creation stories of Genesis were not written down as literal, historical accounts—and that's okay. As we have said, the fact that Genesis 1 is ancient poetry and Genesis 2 is narrative story does not diminish their truth value. Rather, the unique delivery methods provide us with a rich context in which to find the deeper truths within.

The Qur'an 57:3 says, "He is the First and the Last, the Ascendant and the Intimate, and He is, of all things, Knowing." Revelation 1:8 says, "'I am the Alpha and the Omega,' says the Lord God, who is and who was and who is to come, the Almighty." God reveals Himself to us through the Scriptures as the First and the Last. Looking at modern science through the lens of ancient wisdom, we find this revelation truer than ever. The universe, life, and the human mind all begin in imitation of God and will similarly end in the pursuit of His imitation. From beginning to end, from unity to infinity, all things come from God and move toward God. He is both the First and the Final Cause. The entire cosmos is contained within His immensity and His image is written upon it all.

In summary, the creative work of God appears to be this:

> Before time began, God is.
> In the Big Bang, nothingness gave birth to matter.
> In the first cells, matter gave birth to life.
> In the first humans, life gave birth to the immortal soul.
> In the Virgin Birth of Jesus, the immortal soul gave birth to God.

> Each step both natural *and* supernatural.
> Every stage displaying God's oneness, infinity, eternity, and unknowability.
> From God to God. Truly a wonder to behold.

Afterword

Thank you for joining me on this journey through the wonders of philosophy, theology, cosmology, and biology. I hope you've gained some insights from the masters along the way and have hopefully come up with some new ideas of your own. More than that, I hope we have discovered why God and science don't have to live at odds. Rather, the two can and should go together—science revealing the theology in its own way, like two sides of the same coin.

I titled this book *The Call of Wonder* because I believe wonder actively pursues each of us. We are the recipients who need only respond to its call. In that light, I want to encourage you to follow the call of wonder wherever it leads you. I hope you follow it without fear of what you might find in the world of faith as well as in science. I hope you follow its call out into nature and into the beauty of life, that you follow it deep into space and out past the edges of the universe. Follow your wonder inside as well, into the deepest parts of what makes you human. I hope you follow the call of wonder for the rest of your life until it leads you, at last, into the greatest mystery of all.

Staring at the Sun

I'd like to leave you with one final analogy. It is the analogy of our everyday experience of the sun in the sky. Plato was on to something when he used the sun as his example for the Form of the Good. In a way, the sun that shines down on us day after day is one of the best analogies for God.

God is the necessary being who holds all things in existence by sharing His primary existence with them. So, too, the sun does something like this for the world. It is our necessary being for life on Earth. We see by its light and are warmed by its heat. Plants rely on the sun for photosynthesis and animals rely on it for temperature regulation and food supply. Without the sun, life on Earth would quickly cease to be. An analogy of the necessity of God.

God is one, indivisible and perfectly united. Our sun appears to us in this same way. To the eye, it looks to be composed of only one thing—pure, burning light. In technical terms, it is a flaming ball of hydrogen and helium undergoing a massive fusion reaction, but not to our everyday experience. Humans throughout the centuries have looked up into the sky and seen only light. A humble revelation of God's oneness and divine simplicity.

The sun appears circular in shape. Like a wedding band without beginning or end symbolizing eternal love, so the sun's shape has no beginning or end. Cultures and religions throughout history have used circular shapes of all kinds to represent concepts like infinity and eternity. The very shape of the sun in the sky is yet another analogy of God's eternal essence.

The sun moves us without having to do anything at all. As you recall, creatures are moved by the Unmoved Mover out of a desire to be closer to its beauty and perfection. The Unmoved Mover moves us in the direction of our ultimate fulfillment by simply being what it is. So it is with God, we want to be closer to Him and be more like Him. In a similar way, the sun moves the earth by simply being what it is. Its mass bends space-time so that the earth is forever falling into it. We move around the sun by the simple virtue of its presence near to us.

Interestingly, we are unable to look directly at the sun. We can look near it, using our peripheral vision to sort of see it, but if we try to gaze directly into its light, the sheer intensity will blind us. The energy put off by the sun is too great for our eyes to receive— it's quite literally too much to look upon. In this way, it becomes another analogy of God. The Big Bang, the evolution of life, and the human mind all remain something of a mystery. We cannot "see" into them completely. All reminders of the ultimate mystery that is God.

He is present to us at every moment, though we may not always feel that presence. So, too, is the sun in the sky. The sun is faithful; it rises every morning without fail. It is ever present during the day, and at night we know it's there by the reflected light of the moon. Even when clouds block the sun from our view, we know it still exists, faithfully providing light and warmth—a simple revelation of God's continual presence. As Dostoyevsky wrote in *The Brothers Karamazov*, "I see the sun, and if I don't see the sun, I know it's there. And there's a whole life in that, in knowing that the sun is there."[1]

Two Favors to Ask

If you enjoyed this book, I would be exceedingly grateful if you left a review on Amazon.com. Your reviews help authors like me spread our work to as many readers as possible. You can also sign up for my free newsletter at briancranley.com.

Secondly, if you know someone who might benefit from reading a book like this, please share it with them. My goal has always been to pass along the treasure of knowledge that was generously given to me by teachers, family, and friends. If any of these ideas have helped, inspired, or challenged you in any way, perhaps they might also be of help to someone you know.

Thank you sincerely,
—Brian

Acknowledgments

I would first like to thank my family for encouraging me to write my first book. Writing has never come easy for me and I am beyond grateful for your love and support. This book would not have been possible without you.

A special thank you to Janay Garrick and Andy Earle; you taught me early on what writing a book entails and encouraged me to begin it. To my friend Matthew Soetaert who generously read the book at three different stages, your feedback proved invaluable. Thank you Dr. Tim Ratino, Dr. Tom Ratino, Dr. Manny Ybarra, Dr. Ric Alvarado, Tim Watts, and Chris Dawson for reading sections of the book, listening to the ideas, sharing back your perspectives, and challenging me to finish the work. Thank you also, Eve Porinchak and Toby Coley, for your editing expertise and enthusiasm on my early drafts.

Special thanks to my friend Fr. Dean Wilhelm for offering your theological insights and for allowing me to bounce mine off you as well. Thank you, Mom, for your excitement and encouragement on the book. Dad, your own writing and ideas have been a guiding light to help me navigate this path. To my sister, Kristy, who taught me all about the *tohu wa-bohu* during our many late-night discussions, thank you so much. To my sister, Marie, your entrepreneurial spirit and creativity are so inspiring and you have taught me a tremendous amount. And to my brother, Matt, your all-out pursuit of music has encouraged me to make art a priority in my own life.

I am beyond grateful for my work family who generously stepped up to run our territory, allowing me precious time to write. Thank you sincerely to Tom Bannister, April Jukes, Sean Fletcher, and Danielle Carrell. Dr. Ashley Classen, thank you for sharing your theological insights with me and for your support on this project. Dr. E. Jo Bailey and Dr. Ashley Scott Bailey-Classen, thank you both for your friendship, support, and the fantastic gatherings at the ranch.

I would also like to acknowledge Tim Ferriss (tim.blog), Yates & Yates (yates2.com), Reedsy (reedsy.com), and Zach Kristensen (juxtabook.com) for providing invaluable insights and professional guidance on every step of the writing process. Without these (often free) resources, I would never have known how to navigate the writing and publishing journey.

Finally, a huge thank you to Dee Kerr, Benito Salazar, Emma Watson, Jared Dorsey, and my Greenleaf Book Group publishing team for your expert help in getting this book across the finish line and out into the world.

Notes

Introduction

1. C.S. Lewis, *Mere Christianity* (Harper One, 1996), p. viii.
2. National Park Service, "Rocky Mountain," US Department of the Interior, https://www.nps.gov/romo/planyourvisit/upload/keyhole_route_2011a.pdf.

Chapter 1

1. "Stephen Hawking on Religion: 'Science Will Win,'" ABC News, June 4, 2010, https://abcnews.go.com/WN/Technology/stephen-hawking-religion-science-win/story?id=10830164.
2. Stephen Covey, *7 Habits of Highly Effective People* (Simon and Schuster, 2020), pp. 273–296.
3. Leon Festinger, Stanley Schacter, and Henry Riecken, *When Prophecy Fails* (University of Minnesota Press, 1956).
4. Nick Spencer, "Darwin's Religious Beliefs," The Faraday Institute, February 19, 2009.
5. Helmut T. Lehmann and John W. Doberstein, *Luther's Works: Sermons I, Volume 51* (Fortress Press, 1959).

6. Isaac Newton, *The Principia*, trans. Bernard Cohen and Anne Whitman (University of California Press, 1999).

Chapter 2

1. Plato, *The Republic*, Book VI, https://www.gutenberg.org/files/1497/1497-h/1497-h.htm.

2. Plato, *The Republic*, Book VII, https://www.gutenberg.org/files/1497/1497-h/1497-h.htm#link2H_4_0010.

Chapter 3

1. Simon Sinek, *The Infinite Game* (Portfolio/Penguin, 2019).

2. Will Durant, *The Story of Civilization, Volume 2: The Life of Greece* (Blackstone Audio, 2013), audio CD.

3. Aristotle, *Metaphysics*, Book V, trans. John H. McMahon (Prometheus Books, 1991), p. 90.

4. Aristotle, *Metaphysics*, Book XII, trans. McMahon, p. 248.

5. Aristotle, *Physics*, Book IV: 10–14, trans. C.D.C. Reeve (Hackett Publishing Company, 2018), p. 74.

6. Aristotle, *De Caelo*, I.9, 279 a17–30, trans. C.D.C. Reeve (Hackett Publishing Company, 2020).

Chapter 4

1. *Encyclopedia Britannica Online*, s.v. "Library of Alexandria," https://www.britannica.com/topic/Library-of-Alexandria.

2. Will Durant, *The Story of Civilization, Volume 2: The Life of Greece* (Blackstone Audio, 2013), audio CD.

3. John 1:1–3 (NIV).

4. Michael Friedlander, *The Jewish Religion* (P. Vallentine & Son, 1900), pp. 20–21.

5. Maimonides, *The Guide for the Perplexed*, trans. Michael Friedlander, fourth ed. (Dutton, 1904), p. 2.

6. Avicenna Foundation, www.avicennafoundation.org.uk.

7. Richard C. Taylor, *Averroes: Religious Dialectic and Aristotelian Philosophical Thought* (Cambridge University Press, 2005), p. 189.

8. Ibn Rush'd, *Classical Arabic Philosophy: An Anthology of Sources. The Decisive Treatise*, trans. Jon McGinnis and David C. Reisman (Hackett Publishing, 2007), p. 314.

9. Shafique N. Virani, "Taqiyya and Identity in a South Asian Community," *Journal of Asian Studies* 70, no. 1 (2011): 99–139, 131–132.

10. William Paley, *Natural Theology or Evidences of the Existence and Attributes of the Deity* (Cambridge University Press, 1802), pp. 1–2.

11. Augustine, *The City of God*, Book VIII, https://gutenberg.org/files/45304/45304-h/45304-h.htm.

12. Augustine, *Confessions*, trans. Henry Chadwick (Oxford University Press, 1998), p. 228.

13. Augustine, *Confessions*, trans. Chadwick, p. 225.

Chapter 5

1. Thomas Aquinas, *Summa Theologia*, Prima Pars, Q3, A1–2, https://www.gutenberg.org/cache/epub/17611/pg17611-images.html.

2. Aquinas, *Summa Theologia*, Prima Pars, Q3, A1–2, https://www.gutenberg.org/cache/epub/17611/pg17611-images.html.

3. Aquinas, *Summa Theologia*, Prima Pars, Q3, A7, https://www.gutenberg.org/cache/epub/17611/pg17611-images.html.

4. Aquinas, *Summa Theologia*, Prima Pars, Q7, A1, https://www.gutenberg.org/cache/epub/17611/pg17611-images.html.

5. Aquinas, *Summa Theologia*, Prima Pars, Q7, A1, https://www.gutenberg.org/cache/epub/17611/pg17611-images.html.

6. Aquinas, *Summa Theologia*, Prima Pars, Q10, A1–2, https://www.gutenberg.org/cache/epub/17611/pg17611-images.html.

7. Aquinas, *Summa Theologia*, Prima Pars, Q12, A11, https://www.gutenberg.org/cache/epub/17611/pg17611-images.html.

8. Aquinas, *Summa Theologia*, Prima Pars, Q12, A1, https://www.gutenberg.org/cache/epub/17611/pg17611-images.html.

9. Frank Sheed, *A Map of Life* (Ignatius Press, 1994), p. 82.

Chapter 6

1. "Not with a Bang, but a Whisper," APS125, https://www.aps.org/archives/publications/apsnews/200712/letters.cfm.

2. Simon Mitton, "The Expanding Universe of Georges Lemaître," *Astronomy & Geophysics* 58, no. 2 (April 2017): 2.28–2.31, https://academic.oup.com/astrogeo/article/58/2/2.28/3074085.

3. Clara Moskowitz, "Smart Luck: How the Big Bang Was Found by Accident," *Scientific American*, May 30, 2014, https://www.scientificamerican.com/article/smart-luck-how-the-big-bang-was-found-by-accident/.

4. Georges Lemaître, "The Beginning of the World from the Point of View of Quantum Theory," *Nature* 127, no. 706 (1931): https://doi.org/10.1038/127706b0.

5. Katie Mack, *The End of Everything (Astrophysically Speaking)* (Scribner, 2020), pp. 36–37.

6. Nobel Prize, "The Nobel Prize in Physics 2013," https://www.nobelprize.org/prizes/physics/2013/summary/.

7. Nola Taylor Tillman and Scott Dutfield, "How Was the Moon Formed?," Space.com, January 21, 2022, https://www.space.com/19275-moon-formation.html.

8. *Merriam-Webster*, s.v. "analogy," https://www.merriam-webster.com/dictionary/analogy.

9. Mack, *End of Everything*, 88–89.

Chapter 7

1. *Merriam-Webster*, s.v. "abiogenesis," https://www.merriam-webster.com/dictionary/abiogenesis.

2. Henry Gee, *A (Very) Short History of Life on Earth: 4.6 Billion Years in 12 Pithy Chapters* (St. Martin's Press, 2021), pp. 4–5.

3. *Encyclopedia Britannica Online*, s.v. "Miller-Urey experiment," https://www.britannica.com/science/Miller-Urey-experiment.

4. Charles Darwin, *On the Origin of Species by Means of Natural Selection*, J. Carroll, ed. (Broadview Texts, 2003).

5. Keith Cooper, "Looking for LUCA, the Last Universal Common Ancestor," Astrobiology at NASA, March 30, 2017, https://astrobiology.nasa.gov/news/looking-for-luca-the-last-universal-common-ancestor/.

6. National Park Service, "The Pygmy Mammoth," US Department of the Interior, September 22, 2020, https://home.nps.gov/chis/learn/historyculture/pygmymammoth.htm.

7. Martin Nowak, *Beyond* (Angelico Press, 2024), p. 141.

8. Peter Wohlleben, *The Hidden Life of Trees: What They Feel, How They Communicate—Discoveries from a Secret World* (Greystone Books, 2016), p. 3–4.

9. Andy Weir, *Project Hail Mary* (Ballantine Books, 2021).

10. Phillip Johnson, *Darwin on Trial* (InterVarsity Press, 1991).

Chapter 8

1. *Encyclopedia Britannica*, s.v. "Lucy," https://www.britannica.com/topic/Lucy-fossil.

2. Yuval Noah Harari, *Sapiens* (HarperCollins, 2015), p. 9.

3. Jacques Cauvin, *The Birth of the Gods and the Origins of Agriculture* (Cambridge University Press, 2000), p. xv.

4. "Lascaux," Ministère de la Culture, https://archeologie.culture.gouv.fr/lascaux/en.

5. G.K. Chesterton, *The Everlasting Man* (Word on Fire, 2023), pp. 46–47.

6. Aristotle, *De Anima*, 429b29–430a1, trans. C.D.C. Reeve (Hackett Publishing Company, 2017).

7. Sajjad H. Rizvi, *Internet Encyclopedia of Philosophy*, s.v. "Avicenna (Ibn Sina)," https://iep.utm.edu/avicenna-ibn-sina/.

8. John Locke, *Essay Concerning Human Understanding*, Peter H. Nidditch, ed. (Oxford University Press, 1979).

9. Osvaldo Cairó, "External Measures of Cognition," *Frontiers in Human Neuroscience* (2011), https://www.ncbi.nlm.nih.gov/pmc/articles/PMC3207484/.

10. V.S. Ramachandran, *The Tell-Tale Brain: A Neuroscientist's Quest for What Makes Us Human* (Norton & Company, 2011), pp. 4–5.

Chapter 9

1. Joseph Campbell, *The Hero with a Thousand Faces* (MJF Books, 1949), p. 30.

2. Genesis (RSV).

3. William LaSor, David Hubbard, and Frederic Bush, *The Old Testament Survey*, 2nd ed. (William B. Eerdmans Publishing Company, 1996).

4. Edmon Gallagher, *Translation of the Seventy: History, Reception, and Contemporary Uses of the Septuagint* (Abilene Christian University Press, 2021), p. 125.

5. Joseph Ratzinger, *Introduction to Christianity*, trans. Joseph Foster (Ignatius Press, 1990), p. 78.

6. *Plato Complete Works*, John M. Cooper, ed. (Hackett Publishing, 1997), p. 1253.

7. *Plato Complete Works*, p. 1253.

8. Genesis 2:4–25 (RSV).

Chapter 10

1. Genesis 1:28 (RSV).

2. Genesis 2:7 (RSV).

Afterword

1. Fyodor Dostoevsky, *The Brothers Karamazov*, trans. Constance Garnett (Lowell Press, 1912), p. 212.

About the Author

Author photograph by Ellah Laurenn Photography

Throughout his life, Brian Cranley, MDiv, has been fascinated by the intersection of God and the "real world." This led him to earn a BS in biomedical engineering from Texas A&M University and later a master's of divinity from the University of St. Thomas in Houston. Today, he lives in the Texas Hill Country outside San Antonio with his family. When he's not writing, you can find him running a thriving medical device business and spending time with his girls outdoors. In his free time, he continues his own search for wonder in the worlds of philosophy, theology, and science.